The benefits of c   ate, public and
voluntary sectors   d of increasing
complexity, leaders are frequently required to work across conventional boundaries to achieve their objectives. This almost inevitably requires leaders to have the capability to collaborate effectively. In this work McDermott and Hall set out to demystify the art of collaboration and provide a methodology for leaders to achieve excellence in its application. The book also addresses the negative side of failed collaborative ventures and analyses the principle causes. A must-read for aspiring leaders and everyone grappling with complex change.

Martin Roberts PhD, author of
Change Management Excellence

In business, collaborative leadership is becoming an essential skill and principle ... and yet it is often misunderstood, with frustrating results. In *The Collaborative Leader*, the authors give you plenty of thought-provoking questions, examples and models to help you walk the sometimes less than easy path of true collaboration.

Joe Cheal, leadership development specialist and author

Ian and Michael have been great thinkers and creators of quality information for the field of NLP for many years and their latest effort is certainly something special. Collaborative leadership, for most writers, is like trying to organize smoke. Ian and Michael have managed to be systematic, carefully specific (where most have failed), and even pragmatic in this effort to help us all understand, and actually learn how to use, the wonderful and valuable systems of collaboration. I really appreciate their careful explanation that leaders must make sure that their own preconceptions and habits are fully understood and sometimes changed. So, here we have critically important skill sets, presented at the right time in our ongoing effort to help organizations and teams move toward excellence. They have professionally identified principles and skills in a way that is pragmatic enough to be incredibly useful. Right information, right time, right presenters. It doesn't get better. Get the book and find out for yourself what a sterling job these two men have done, again.

R. Frank Pucelik, Pucelik Consulting Group,
INLPTA, and ANLP

the
collaborative
leader

The ultimate leadership challenge

Ian McDermott and L. Michael Hall PhD

Crown House Publishing Limited
www.crownhouse.co.uk

First published by

Crown House Publishing Ltd
Crown Buildings, Bancyfelin, Carmarthen, Wales, SA33 5ND, UK
www.crownhouse.co.uk

and

Crown House Publishing Company LLC
PO Box 2223, Williston, VT 05495
www.crownhousepublishing.com

First published 2016. Reprinted 2017.

Cover image iStock.com/Mark Airs

British Library Cataloguing-in-Publication Data
A catalogue entry for this book is available
from the British Library.

Print ISBN 978-178583009-9
Mobi ISBN 978-178583054-9
ePub ISBN 978-178583055-6
ePDF ISBN 978-178583056-3

LCCN 2015953354

Printed and bound in the UK by
Gomer Press, Landysul, Ceredigion

Contents

Preface

Behind all the current buzz about collaboration is a discipline. And with all due respect to the ancient arts of governing and diplomacy, the more recent art of collaboration does represent something new—maybe Copernican. If it contained a silicon chip, we'd all be excited.

John Gardner

Creative collaboration is now possible on an unprecedented scale, by people based all over the world.

Warren Bennis, *On Becoming a Leader* (2003)

Collaboration is co-laboring, literally "laboring with" others. Given this, it is only natural that a book on collaboration should be written collaboratively by more than one author. That's precisely what we have done in this book.

Both of us have engaged in many collaborations over the years and we ascribe much of our personal success to working with others—collaborating. We are also both seasoned writers as well as leaders in our own areas. Did we have time to collaborate and write another book? No, but we made time because this really matters to us, which is true of many collaborations.

When we began there was another person involved in this project—Shelle Rose Charvet. Actually, she was the one who originally brought us together and the three of us worked on this project jointly. But then "life happens" and Shelle realized she had taken on too much and needed to focus on her new business. She said that "for my own well-being I need to cut back on my commitments." So she chose to step out of the project. This made us aware of an important aspect of collaboration: Collaborations inevitably grow, change, and evolve as people, situations, and needs shift over time.

As our experience with Shelle makes clear, collaboration is a rich and dynamic process between people; it is a living, evolving experience. It is not a rigid set of roles or rules about how to do something. It is an act and experience of creativity wherein a few, or many, people discover how to interact in such a way that new emergent ideas arise; ideas which, when put into action, can bring forth new and wonderful innovations.

"Can You Give Me the 'TED Version' of This Book?"

While we identified a great many facets of collaboration in our initial inquiry phase, when we began writing this book, we shifted our focus to a singular question: What do we feel passionate about regarding collaboration that would make this book unique and transformative for the lives of those who read it?

In this book we have answered that question by focusing on three main considerations about collaboration and leadership:

1. What is collaboration?
2. How does it relate to leadership?
3. How do you do it effectively?

First, what is collaboration? Collaboration is the demanding business of working together to get things done in order to get practical results. It builds businesses, makes money, and launches pragmatic solutions into the world. As we show you how this works, you will see how it can give you an edge in your leadership.

Second, how does collaboration relate to leadership? Collaboration requires leadership. It needs a person (or team) to bring people together and enable them to work effectively as one. Inspiring and administrating a collaborative partnership brings out the best in them. As we explain how to do this, you will learn lots of collaborative leadership skills.

Third, how do you do collaboration effectively? Collaboration necessitates skills. It requires a set of core competencies that enable people to work together effectively to achieve what none could accomplish alone or apart. As you develop these qualities, you will take your leadership skills to a whole new level.

We have found that there are many misconceptions about collaboration. One of the most common is that collaboration is a nice idea about people getting along and feeling good about each other, but it doesn't improve the bottom line. Another myth is that collaboration requires a mediator, not a leader, because it involves getting people to compromise. There are many more. Such myths obscure the fact that collaboration actually gives businesses a competitive advantage and can deliver a real return on investment. All truly great organizations are great because of collaboration. We call these misconceptions *collaboration myths*.

Our contention is that a great deal of collaboration is hidden in plain sight and its importance is often unrecognized and unappreciated. Without some degree of implicit collaboration, it's almost impossible to get much done at all. We believe this has huge implications for anyone in leadership. As you will discover, the fact is that collaboration involves a set of core competencies that are, in effect, leadership competencies. These can be learned and improved.

This also highlights another hidden truth: The ability to collaborate is the ultimate leadership skill. And that's what our world is increasingly demanding—collaborative leaders. Therefore, promoting collaboration as a skill set is the next great step in leadership development. So, we have written this book to make explicit what collaborative leadership is and how to become that kind and quality of leader.

What Will You Get From This Book?

There are many benefits to be gained. First of all, a practical approach to developing high level collaboration skills. Instead of focusing on the theories behind collaboration, we have designed *The Collaborative Leader* to be a guide for how to collaborate with others and how to be a collaborative leader. This means learning how to win the hearts and minds of those you lead. Only then will people participate in a collaborative vision with you. You will find assessment questions throughout, step-by-step processes on collaboration, and an invitation to action at the end of each chapter under the title, "Your Next Steps In Being a Collaborative Leader."

Second, practical and immediate things to do. We have organized the book so you can immediately begin testing the usefulness of the ideas—perhaps even turnaround a non-collaborative group or environment.

Third, a personal challenge to step up to the collaborative level of leadership. To lead others is to steer them to work together and to combine their intellectual and relational capital. As a leader you lead them to collaborate. That's why the leader who cannot effectively collaborate cannot effectively lead. If you are to walk your talk, you need to demonstrate collaborative skills yourself.

Fourth, a model of the structure of collaboration. We come from a field that specializes in modeling expertise and excellence—neuro-linguistic programming (NLP). We began our own collaboration by unpacking (i.e., modeling) examples of collaboration—what made them work, what the challenges were, how collaborators dealt with barriers to collaboration, the beliefs and values of the collaborators, and much more. By the end of this book, you will have a thorough understanding of the structure and processes of collaboration.

Fifth, a guide to the set of competencies that facilitate a healthy, joyful, and productive collaboration. One of the things we discovered in the process of studying collaboration is that the best collaborators are those individuals who have lots of fun collaborating. The goal can be serious; the collaboration can be fun. People repeatedly speak of the pleasure they derive from collaborating, how it brings out the best in others, and how on occasion the experience takes on the qualities of a classic flow state—lost in the moment, with a strong sense of meaningfulness, joy, challenge, and effortlessness.

Sixth, the "how to's" for developing the critical success elements of leadership. There is one thing that perhaps makes this book unique: In contrast to the majority of books about collaboration, we focus on the individual collaborative leader. Most titles in this field are about organizations collaborating with organizations and how to create inter-organizational collaboration.

Seventh, a personal taking stock. It's tough to promote collaboration with and between others if you're at war within yourself. Getting your own behavior aligned with your own values is part of the secret of being an effective collaborative leader. The foundation of collaborative leadership is self-collaboration. It begins with you because high quality collaboration is an inside-out process. What, you may ask, is self-collaboration? It's the ability to collaborate with the different aspects of yourself. We will return to this element continuously throughout the book.

So, are you a collaborative leader? Would you like to be? Do you know how to pull people together, inspire them with a meaningful vision, and organize them so that a team spirit emerges and can deliver peak performance? If you would like to say "yes" to these questions, then this book is definitely for you.

Ian McDermott
L. Michael Hall

Part I

The Foundations of Collaborative Leadership— Leading the Call

Chapter 1
The Vision

Why Bother?

Collaboration will be the point of differentiation between the companies that grow successfully into the next decade and those that don't.

Neil McPhail, CEO of Best Buy

Successful collaboration is the science of the possible.

Warren Bennis and Patricia Ward Biederman,
Organizing Genius: The Secrets Of
Creative Collaboration (1998)

As a leader, why bother with collaboration? What is in it for you and for those you lead? Consider any of the truly great achievements that human beings have created—the pyramids of Egypt, the Great Wall of China, nations uniting to stop Hitler, putting a man on the moon, building sky-scrapers in modern cities. When you do so, you are contemplating acts of collaboration. People came together, worked together, shared a vision, and achieved what would have been impossible alone or apart. Because of a collaborative effort the incredible happened. This is the magic of collaboration.

Or think of the great corporations that exist today—those in the auto industry (Toyota, Volkswagen, General Motors, etc.), the IT industry (Microsoft, Apple, Google, etc.), banking (JPMorgan Chase, HSBC Holdings, Citigroup, etc.), and so on. When you do, you are contemplating acts of collaboration—human beings operating as collaborative partners.

So collaboration is good for the bottom line of profit *and* it is also good for the other two bottom lines of highly successful companies—people and passion. In other words, via collaboration you can create synergy out of the dichotomy between what many people think of as opposites—the hard side and the soft side of business. Collaboration can actually solve many of the problems which businesses suffer today, such as a one-sided overemphasis on money as the sole criteria of corporate success. Money is important but it is not the sole purpose of commerce. Business also requires a focus on people; it requires responsible, ethical, cooperative individuals. This saves companies from suffering from a silo mentality, indulging in unethical business practices, sacrificing people for the return on investment (ROI), and so on.

At its best, a collaborative vision unleashes hidden and untapped potentials which, in turn, can create a better world for all. Collaboration facilitates a broader vision for work, organizations, and corporations which transcends just profit. Collaboration also enables good people to be great together. The very experience of collaboration changes us. It changes how we relate in our work environments and it changes the business and political cultures we have inherited. Through collaboration we can also tap into emergent expressions of creativity that put us, and our organizations, on the cutting edge of innovation, leading us to pioneering new products, services, and information.

The collaborative vision is about *who we are together* and *the quality of the way we relate*. Collaboration therefore expands what we do and the results that we create together. Potentially, it also expands the quality of our relationships. Here, then, are two great benefits from collaboration. First, we are able to achieve results together that we cannot achieve alone. Second, the quality of our group experience—the culture that results—gives us both a competitive advantage as well as a community of which we can enjoy being a part.

Fostering collaboration also addresses one of the most destructive problems troubling all businesses and organizations—disengagement. Employees who are not engaged in the business—who are bored, resistant, and disloyal—are people who cost the company. They are also dangerous people—a danger to the group spirit, to creativity, and to sustainability. A collaborative culture changes this. Work becomes more engaging because of the quality of our relationships in the workplace and the quality of the teamwork.

When you get people truly caring, connecting, and working together, all kinds of creative ideas and projects emerge. Sometimes this means that individuals begin to have a sense of how they can access their higher values, such as making a difference in the world or contributing to the larger good. When this happens, more is unleashed—and this can take an organization to a whole new level.

The Power of Collaboration

There is an incredible power in collaboration. Human history has demonstrated repeatedly how we can do so much more together than alone or apart. Single heroic leaders are nothing if they cannot foster collaboration.

The power of collaboration has brought about this age of science, technology, space exploration, the social media, and so on. Consider the incredible immensity of the collaboration at CERN in Geneva, Switzerland.[1] CERN, the official name for the European Organization for Nuclear Research, is a large-scale international collaboration of people from seventy countries working together. Palestinians and Israelis working side by side. Iranian and Iraqi scientists working together. All in all, there are more than 2,000 staff members and up to 13,000 people can be on site at any one time.

If collaboration enables science, technology, the arts, and civilization, what then is collaboration? Collaboration is people working together in a partnership to create something that no one individual can create or do single-handedly. This very special state, and state of mind, is about far more than just complying with authority. It is about positively and actively wanting and acting in unity with others to achieve a common goal.

If collaboration refers to working with others, then the opposite is going it alone—the drive for independence, separation, and stepping out alone when no one else believes in our vision. The fascinating thing about human beings is that every one of us feels the pull of both of these forces; they are built into our neurology and psychology. We want to be independent *and* we want to be a part of a community. We want to be true to our innermost self *and* we want to be part of a winning team.

We all begin life within a collaboration, inasmuch as we begin in a family, a community, a town, a nation. Without others, we wouldn't survive at all. All of our basic human needs are met by others. After that begins the developmental pull within us to separate, to individuate, to become a self in our own right, to define ourselves, to find our own way. This instigates the individuation process of childhood and the teenage years as we gradually become independent adults. But, at the same time, we feel yet another urge

---

1   CERN is home to the Large Hadron Collider (LHC), set in a 27 kilometer circumference circular tunnel located 100 meters underground, which cost multiple billions to construct.

emerging—the social urge, the pull to be a part of a group, to have close friends, to find a special one to love, to become interdependent.

> No man is an island, entire of itself; every man is a piece of the continent, a part of the main.
>
> **John Donne, Meditation XVII,**
> ***Devotions Upon Emergent Occasions* (1623)**

The pull of collaboration arises because we are social beings with social needs—for love and affection, for bonding, for companionship, to have colleagues, to be a part of a winning team, to be recognized by peers, to count in their eyes. Yet so many things can mess up this drive. Lots of people are blocked from creative collaborations because of their desire to have things "their way" or because of their need for constant recognition and attention.

Others are blocked from effective collaborations because they haven't learned basic social skills: listening, supporting, validating, confirming, and taking time to be present. They didn't learn the lessons of kindergarten—how to play well with others. They are bossy, demanding, self-centered, critical, sarcastic, and unkind. They are not good team players. There are many other blocks that interfere with effective collaboration: fear of change, vested interest in the status quo, fear of loss of self in a group, inability to be a part of a community, lack of vision, and intolerance. We will cover these in the coming chapters.

Nonetheless, in today's interconnected world, collaboration is more important than ever. Neither individuals nor nations can afford to go it alone, operate in isolation, or act independently from the rest of the world. Realizing "big hairy audacious goals" requires people working together effectively as high performance teams.

Nowadays, companies are moving toward self-managing teams who collaboratively provide leadership and management for an area of responsibility. In order to move to this level of high performance, we need to have self-actualizing individuals—people who want (and know how) to operate as part of a high performance team. They need to know how to tap into each other's unique differences and enable others to be an important part of the group. To facilitate this, we need collaborative leadership—leaders who have the ability to set a vision, pioneer with a collaborative style, pull people together, and work through the conflict of differences so that a group spirit emerges.

Some of the most successful companies are the result of collaborative partnerships—individuals working together for mutual benefit. It is our belief that those who do not develop this personal power will be left behind.

What Is Collaboration?

For a clear definition of collaboration we begin with the word itself: *co-* (with) and *labor* (work). An operational definition for collaboration is:

- Working intelligently with other people for a mutual vision and benefit.
- A form of co-leadership, with people working together as partners, which brings out the best in everyone and achieves results that a single person could not have accomplished alone.
- Learning from each other, sharing knowledge freely, helping each other to complete jobs and meet deadlines, and sharing resources for a common good.
- Tapping into differences to create the required synergy that solves problems.
- Working together as a team rather than as disconnected individuals.
- The ability to pull together to actualize a shared vision or solve a problem, and innovate a new solution.

In collaboration, two or more persons come together to combine their understanding, skills, and resources to achieve a richer and fuller outcome than any one person could achieve single-handedly. This means that collaboration is a creative way of interacting and connecting with others which encourages fun, ingenuity, and resourcefulness. Where there is true collaboration, there is a creative synergy of differences. That synergy both unifies and enables individuals to experience an intense and high level of resourcefulness in ideas and actions and, as a result, surprising and unprecedented results often occur.

How Much Collaboration Do You Want?

All collaboration is not the same, neither in nature and character, nor in degree. We use a continuum to help people determine how much collaboration they consider appropriate. Our experience is that people find these distinctions very useful. The continuum ranges from competition to synergy:

Competition	Compliance	Coordination
Compete against others	Passively go along; put up with leaders or group	Organize time and efforts to coordinate activity
Cooperation	**Collaboration**	**Synergy**
Seek to work together in a good spirit	Share a vision of possibilities; team spirit is best for everyone	Tap into unique differences for synthesis

Types of Collaborations

Determining what type of collaboration is optimal is equally useful. Here are six kinds to consider:

1. *Ad hoc collaborations*: People coming together for a limited time to work together on a project or problem and then disband.
2. *Long-term collaborations*: Teams, committees, and boards (usually a permanent structure within an organization); partners in personal life.
3. *Crisis collaborations*: People coming together to resolve an unexpected crisis who become an emergency team.
4. *Interpersonal collaborations*: Group of individuals working together for a common vision.
5. *Inter-organizational collaborations*: Two or more organizations working together on a common problem or vision.
6. *Leader-driven collaborations*: Individual leader who convenes others to work with him or her to achieve a vision.

The Benefits of Collaboration

Some of the key benefits of collaboration include:

- *Larger challenges*: Collaboration enables us to take on challenges that are too big for a single individual.
- *Larger results*: Collaboration facilitates us to accomplish things together that we could not accomplish alone or apart from others, and this unleashes extra potential.
- *Increased return on investment*: High quality collaboration increases the ROI in organizations.
- *Managing risk*: Managed well, collaboration can reduce risk and the fears which accompany it.
- *Competitive advantage*: Many cutting-edge companies today are gaining competitive advantage from harnessing the power of collaboration. They access more talent to increase the synergies which favor innovation.
- *Facing uncertainty*: Collaboration enables us to face the uncertainty and ambiguity which is required for creativity, as we have each other to depend upon.
- *Vitality*: Collaboration enables us to have more fun at work, to be more playful and optimistic, adding an *élan vital* to the organization.
- *Fun*: Collaboration enables groups and teams to experience greater levels of creativity and fun.
- *Learning*: Collaboration promotes group or team learning which transcends individual learning.
- *Quality relationships*: Collaboration enriches the quality of relationships at work and lowers attrition, thereby retaining the best people.
- *High quality culture*: Collaboration enriches the kind of culture in organizations that increases the quality of creative products and services.
- *Teamwork*: Collaborations can inspire people to want to be part of a group, team, or organization.
- *Unleashing potential*: Collaboration facilitates the unleashing of potential in all of the participants.
- *New gestalts*: Collaboration can unleash a synergy to create outcomes that are far more than the sum of their parts.
- *Emotional intelligence*: Collaboration can enhance trust and emotional intelligence so there is more self-management, self-leadership, maturity, and sense of responsibility.

- *Inspiration*: Collaboration increases inspiration and motivation as we work on something larger than ourselves. It improves morale.
- *Resilience*: Collaboration makes us more resilient because we have others who can hold us up when the going gets tough.
- *Humane organizations*: Collaboration enables us to make our work life more and humane. This reduces stress, disengagement, theft, etc.
- *Creativity*: According to John Briggs, "Collaboration is one of the best kept secrets in creativity."

The average return on collaboration is nearly four times a company's initial investment.
   Ricci and Wiese, *The Collaborative Imperative* (2011)

How Do You Do It?

While collaboration may have many benefits, it takes leadership to create and foster effective collaboration. It does not happen without intentional leadership, and it often takes determined leadership with a vision and an attitude. In particular, it takes leaders who are especially skilled in handling conflict and differences.

Collaboration requires men and women who initiate, inspire, and guide the process. That is because to be collaborative is itself an act of leadership. Whenever anyone pulls others together to undertake a shared project or vision, they are demonstrating leadership. Collaborative leadership requires the ability to see possibilities despite conflict, barriers, silo thinking, and giant egos. For a leader to step up to become a collaborative leader is to "man up" to such challenges, whether the leader is a man or a woman.

Leading Collaboration

Leadership is, by its very nature, the process of enabling people to work together effectively. What then is a *collaborative leader*? A collaborative leader is someone who is able to get people to work effectively together for the sake of greater productivity and efficiency.

That's not easy. It doesn't happen in a moment. It takes time. How does this work? How does a leader create this level and quality of collaboration? To achieve this, leaders develop the inspiration and the know-how for getting people to cooperate to produce a team effort. An effective leader has what may be considered a "magical gift"—namely, that of enabling individuals to work together in ways that bring out the best in people, so that everyone wins and everyone enjoys the process.

A collaborative leader also needs to be able to confront people on non-collaborative behavior while inviting them to step up to and engage in a higher quality of collaboration. The collaborative leader sees beyond parochial politics and insulated silos. He or she dares to challenge people to communicate their differences and let them become sources of creativity.

If you don't think that's magical, consider for a moment those who lack this leadership ability. The sad fact is that not everyone who is rewarded with leadership is able to facilitate collaboration. Many leaders behave in ways that trigger others to take sides and waste their energy in conflict. They hold secrets, play favorites, and set faction against faction to manipulate situations to their own benefit. Not only do people not collaborate, they barely cooperate. Playing this kind of politics undermines collaboration.

What is the secret of creating collaboration among people? What are the leadership qualities and skills that enable some leaders to be so effective in fostering collaboration? What are the premises, beliefs, values, and understandings in leaders who are able to bring others together, inspire them with a vision beyond themselves, and organize things so that people love cooperating and have lots of fun being part of a winning team? We will address these critical questions in the following chapters.

Consider the problems and headaches of doing the opposite. What happens when a leader cannot inspire and organize for collaboration? Organizational problems, management problems, labor problems, financial problems, poor efficiency, conflict, stress, loss of revenue, scandals, corruption, and so on. Also, in most companies today, the capital of the business is no longer buildings, bank accounts, and machinery; it is people. We talk in terms of intellectual capital, creative capital, and relational capital. This is another reason to model leaders who are able to create effective collaborations.

Deepening Our Understanding of Collaboration

On the surface, the idea of collaboration sounds simple and direct. In reality, it is a very rich and dynamic experience—one that involves many factors. In researching this book, we have identified many of the necessary facets and factors of successful collaboration.

1. Collaboration requires skills. As you pull people together, you will have to deal with conflicts which difference evokes in individuals. Collaboration emerges when people come together to share a common vision and are organized so they can contribute their best for a team effort. We should not frame collaboration as a touchy-feely thing; collaboration is actually a hard-nosed skill.

2. Collaboration calls for a win-win proposition that everyone understands and buys into. To lead a collaborative team, everybody in the group must feel they are winning. Contrast this with the competitive attitude whereby someone tries to win at another's expense. Rivals seek to gain an advantage over each other or take revenge on a colleague who is succeeding. The opposite of collaborative thinking is the idea of scarcity (i.e., there is not enough for everybody; it's a zero-sum game—win or lose) or transaction-type interactions (where one person exploits or uses another for his or her own purpose).

3. Collaboration begins with self-collaboration. The foundation of collaboration with others is collaboration with yourself. When it comes to collaborating, we can work with single individuals, an entire group, or as part of a group with other groups. Self-collaboration means you are reasonably integrated and not driven by internal conflicts. This emotional good health enables you to reach out in collaboration to others. We might say: Only the strong can collaborate.

4. All collaborations are not the same. As you will discover, there are different degrees and intensities of collaboration. It can involve a range of behaviors from coordinating activities, cooperating in a project or activity, engaging heart and mind in a vision, or investing in something bigger than oneself.

5. Collaboration is so natural that you are already doing it. Collaborating is all about relating to others and it is fundamental to successful living. Ask yourself: Where am I

already collaborating and with whom? Where do I collaborate in my private life? In my career?

6. Collaboration involves a range of behaviors. These range from low level to medium level to high level interactions. The words we typically use to describe these different levels are coordinating, cooperating, engaging (collaborating) and committed.

7. Effective collaboration requires a set of core competencies. The skills of collaboration are high level relational skills. Trying to collaborate without emotional intelligence (EQ) and social intelligence (SQ), by relying on some trick, will not work in the long run. People may regard such behavior as inauthentic and even manipulative.

8. Effective collaboration produces measurable results. We collaborate for a purpose—namely, to achieve an objective. We do it to get results which can be quantified. Without collaboration you will either overwhelm yourself with all that has to be done to achieve something world class or you will reduce your objective to something mediocre.

9. Collaboration enhances the quality of your life and self-confidence. When collaboration is done well, it enriches the life experience of each person in the collaboration. It expands their vision about what is possible and it enables them to experience being part of a winning team. Collaboration enables us to rise above mediocrity and achieve amazing things.

10. Collaboration requires strong leadership—leadership with an edge. Collaboration demands a special kind of leadership. However, unlike the "strong-man" form of leadership (e.g., the hero, the command-and-control kingpin), collaborative leadership is functional and situational, which means that the person who is best suited for leading or giving guidance steps up to the plate.

11. Collaboration is multidimensional—that is, collaboration occurs at various levels. First of all there is an individual collaborating with one or more individuals. Then there is collaboration between individuals and a group (collaborating as a good team member). Beyond that there is collaboration between groups. Generally, if you can't collaborate one to one, it's highly unlikely that you can advance to one-to-a-group or group-to-group collaboration.

In conclusion, the most essential ingredient of leadership is the ability to collaborate and create collaborative partnerships. Fostering teamwork is a necessary skill for anyone who aspires to be an effective leader. If you want anything more than mere compliance—that is, if you want to win the minds and hearts of people—you have to collaborate with them. Command-and-control leadership will not generate a team spirit or a collaborative style. What are the consequences if you do not develop your collaborative knowledge and skills? You undermine your ability to lead, and you undercut the desire of people to want to follow your lead and be a part of your vision.

Your Next Steps In Being a Collaborative Leader

Assume you are on your own collaboration journey as you read each chapter in the book. Create your own collaborative leadership steps by writing down two or three of the most important ideas that you will take away from each one. Then ask yourself, "Given these ideas, what difference could they make in my life?" Write down one or two things that you could actually do.

As you begin this journey, here are some starter questions for you to ponder:

- Do you know how to effectively collaborate with others?
- Are you collaborative in your nature and style?
- Do you enjoy the process of collaborating with others?
- Do you know how to be an effective team player?

Chapter 2
The Mirror

Where Are You?

The goal of collaboration is not collaboration itself, but great results.

Morten Hansen, *Collaboration* **(2009)**

Where are you currently as a collaborative leader? Given that you now know what collaboration is and what it can do, and given that you know it has tremendous power to unleash potential and possibility, we've designed this chapter so that you can take stock of the challenges you may need to address.

If the future belongs to the collaborative, then learning to collaborate will enable you to be a leader of the future. Furthermore, because collaboration enables people to bring their differences and conflicts together in a synergy which facilitates creativity and innovation, your business will become increasingly collaborative and successful in the future.

Collaboration is the best way to get things done which cannot be accomplished alone. To make this practical, this chapter gives you the opportunity to take stock by completing a personal collaboration assessment.

You As a Collaborative Leader

How is your image as a collaborative leader? If you stood in front of a mirror for this personal collaborative assessment, what sort of image would it reflect? Is collaboration an essential part of your style? Do others see you as a collaborative leader? What does the mirror reveal? Ask yourself:

- Am I a collaborative person?
- How does collaboration or competition balance out in my personality?

- Where am I right now in terms of being a collaborative leader?
- What are my next steps in becoming a collaborative leader?

This chapter focuses on seven key questions. These will enable you to explore areas of collaboration and provide you with a profile of yourself and of your ability to collaborate.

1. How confident and secure am I in extending myself to others in order to collaborate?
2. Am I flexible enough to adapt to others in order to allow something greater to emerge, or do I have to do things my way?
3. Can I let go of my way for the greater good of the group, or am I entrenched in having to do things in my own way?
4. If I truly didn't care who got the credit, how would I proceed and interact with other people?
5. Can I keep my eye on the larger outcome, or do I get stuck at the level of positions, postures, and content?
6. Do I clearly distinguish a means (or instrumental value) from an end value?
7. How much does it matter to me that those with whom I'm collaborating are able to win as well as I can win?

1. Personal Confidence: How confident and secure am I in extending myself to others in order to collaborate?

At first blush, collaboration strikes many as so natural, so inevitable, and so required that we naively ask, "Why can't we all just get along?" What is it with us humans that we struggle so much just to get along with each other? Why all the competition, the battles, the conflict, and the wars?

Collaboration is as challenging as it is desirable and productive, and for this reason it can at times seem scary. What makes collaboration challenging? Generally it requires some maturity and personal development to enter into a shared and mutual relationship of give and take. Yet this is what collaboration requires. To play this larger game you need to be confident that you have something unique to bring to the collaboration and that you are not insecure and self-doubting. Another's competition, even superiority, is not a threat to your own value.

When you collaborate you can no longer be the "great leader" or the "lone ranger." You cannot claim all the credit for a great success. You have to share it. The danger is that if you do not have a solid sense of yourself—solid enough so that you can get your ego out of the way—you will not be able to collaborate or enjoy seeing others grow and succeed.

This initial question raises two distinct issues. The first is about your ability or skill. Are you confident that you are able, have the know-how, and the skills to collaborate? Are you certain that you can translate that knowledge into action? The second issue has to do with how collaboration, and the skills of collaborating, affects your sense of self. Are you confident that you are able to extend yourself to others, to cooperate and work with them?

With these two aspects, we can create a model with two axes: willingness and ability.

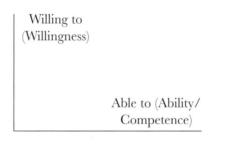

This presents us with two very different requirements for developing the self as a collaborative leader. One has to do with learning the skills of collaboration and the other has to do with learning how to trust (or perhaps to trust again).

So, go ahead and gauge yourself on a continuum of 0 to 10 on your confidence. Put a check mark (√) where you would be (your bias). If it could move around in different contexts include some brackets to indicate the range.

	Wanting to (willingness)	
Unwillingness		Willingness
0	5	10

This also gives you a way to take stock of some different possible combinations. Outlining these is often useful for promoting team discussions as well as self-assessment. As you look at the different potentialities, see which fit for you and also whether any of these descriptions fit anyone you know.

<table>
<tr><td rowspan="2">Desire to Collaborate
High

Low</td><td>I have the willingness, but not the ability</td><td>I have both the willingness and the ability</td></tr>
<tr><td>I have neither the willingness nor ability</td><td>I have the ability, but not the willingness</td></tr>
<tr><td></td><td>Low</td><td>High</td></tr>
</table>

Ability to Collaborate

2. Flexibility: Am I flexible enough to adapt to others in order to allow something greater to emerge, or do I have to do things my way?

This question identifies one of the prerequisites for collaboration—being able to adapt to others. The contrast to this is being rigid and stuck in your ways. Rigidity may take the form of a personal kind of dogmatism, even fundamentalism, as expressed in the bumper sticker: "My way or the highway." What drives rigidity? The answer is either/or thinking. This thinking style presents our choices in a black-or-white format which assumes that there are only two choices available. This kind of dichotomy puts us on the horns of a dilemma: "This or that! Which shall it be?"

The flexibility to adapt means being able to walk a mile in another person's shoes and try on their point of view. Being able to adjust to other people attests to a basic social and relational skill that, ideally, we learned as children—learning how to play well together. This usually involves engaging in some give and take. What is needed to do this, whether as children or as adults, is the emotional intelligence for consideration and empathy.

Here are some questions to ask yourself about your flexibility:

- When I engage with others in a work-related activity, on a community project, or on an adventure with others who share common values and vision, how much flexibility do I have to adapt to others?
- Do I operate from an unconscious assumption that "my way" is obviously the right way or the best way?
- Do I feel put off or disrespected when people want to do things in a way that differs from my way?
- Do I get irritated and annoyed and feel as if I want to move away from the social interaction and just do it myself?
- Once I recognize that there are different ways and that the majority of others want to go with an option that differs from mine, how much flexibility can I show at that point?

Gauge yourself on the following continuum from 0 to 10:

Stubborn/rigid		Adaptable/flexible
0	5	10

3. The Greater Good: Can I let go of my way for the greater good of the group, or am I entrenched in having to do things in my own way?

Do you think in terms of a larger goal or a greater good beyond yourself? This is the point at which differing minds and hearts come together and have to choose one way forward. Do you dig your heels in and become entrenched ("It has to be my way"), or can you let go of your way for the greater good of the group?

This choice between stubbornness and compliance isn't an either/or choice. There are a multitude of positions with degrees of stubbornness and compliance.

Ask yourself the following questions:

- Do I get stuck in a stubborn position that I cling to as if that position was my god, or can I think in terms of the greater good for everybody in the group/family/company/organization?
- Do I take the time and trouble to communicate my intentions and listen for others' intentions?
- Do I engage sufficiently in a conversation so that I can adequately describe the points of view of others, or do I operate from my assumptions about what they understand and are attempting to do?
- Do we as a group of people have a vision of a common good that we share?
- Do we find it a sufficiently inspiring and big enough vision to call forth our best?

Gauge yourself on the following continuum from 0 to 10:

I focus only on my good/ It has to be my way		I also focus on the greater good/ I can and will adapt to others
0	5	10

4. Recognition and Acclaim: If I truly didn't care who got the credit, how would I proceed and interact with other people?

Some of the greatest barriers to collaboration are pride, ego, and the desire for individual recognition, so this question gets to the heart of your personal feelings regarding collaborative endeavors and how much your ego investment gets in the way.

Suppose we could set aside who gets recognized, who gets the credit and the glory, and whose name is on the product, how would you proceed? How would you treat the others in the group and interact with them? If you have a solid sense of yourself, you will see these as opportunities to move forward. A strong sense of your own self-value (or self-esteem) will enable you to stay focused on your long-term goal. This does not mean that you will never struggle with wanting to get some credit— you're human, after all. A secure sense of self is not an on-off switch, so that once switched on you'll never struggle again. What it does mean is that you are much more likely to rise to the occasion as needed.

As an aside, self-esteem is not the same as self-confidence. Self-esteem relates to who you *are* as a person, while self-confidence relates to what you can *do* (as a human doing) and your confidence in what you can do. It is the combination of these two facets of self which enable you to have a strong sense of identity and be ready for healthy collaboration. Paradoxically, it takes a lot of self-esteem to be humble because your sense of dignity, value, worth, and importance are not at risk if you don't get your way on a particular project.

Gauge yourself on the following continuum from 0 to 10:

I want to get the credit		I don't care about the credit
0	5	10

5. Vision: Can I keep my eye on the larger outcome, or do I get stuck at the level of positions, postures, and content?

What causes some people to get lost in the smaller details, such that they miss out on the main point, is that they get caught up in a position. Then, while in the process of winning a battle, they lose the war. By taking a drug that banishes all the symptoms of an illness, they poison themselves with something more potent and become addicted or die.

This question focuses on your ability to keep your eye on the larger outcome of the collaboration—the vision that inspires and excites—rather than specific steps and positions along the way. One barrier to high quality collaboration is getting blinded by a transitory issue that somehow takes control of your allegiances, such that the larger collaborative vision gets lost in the process.

Gauge yourself on the following continuum from 0 to 10:

Doesn't see benefits		Sees benefits
Gets caught up in		Keeps larger
positions		outcome in mind

| 0 | 5 | 10 |

---

6. Ends and Means: Do I clearly distinguish a means (or instrumental value) from an end value?

To what extent do you lose sight of the vision and overall purpose of a project and get caught up in the righteousness of a particular methodology? How flexible can you be, especially when your favorite method is being questioned?

This question about means and ends is similar to question 5 about vision. "Beginning with the end in mind" (Covey, 1989) and holding in mind that end as your vision, allows you to identify the means that will take you there. These means are instrumental processes. They are a means, not the end. They are instrumental values, not end values.

While this may seem like a simple and obvious distinction, it is when we confuse them that we overvalue a means and become seduced into treating it as an end value. When this happens we can become rigid and dogmatic about what should be recognized as an instrumental process. At this point we take a position about how to do something and, frequently, we make it so important that we sacrifice the larger vision for it. Now we have to face the question of our willingness to work through differences and conflicts for the sake of the collaboration.

Gauge yourself on the following continuum from 0 to 10:

Focus on means as most important		Focus on means in service of ends
0	5	10

7. Mutual Win-Win: How much does it matter to me that those with whom I'm collaborating are able to win as well as I can win?

Collaboration involves working together in such a way that we jointly jeopardize our time, effort, money, and personnel. Given this level of risk, if there is not a commitment to a win-win arrangement, then things can go wrong very quickly. This can happen if you think that someone else is getting the best stuff or more stuff than you.

Unethical and ineffective competition arises from a fear of others and lack of self-confidence, and it leads to win-lose competitiveness. You are now in a zero-sum game and this undermines the collaboration. It will poison the spirit of the adventure and stand as a formidable barrier to collaboration.

So, regarding mutual benefit, do you think win-win? Are you willing to champion the idea of win-win and check that everyone is experiencing a win?

Gauge yourself on the following continuum from 0 to 10:

Win-lose		Win-win
0	5	10

Your Collaborative Score

How did you do? Using these simple assessment questions, where do you currently find yourself in terms of collaboration? Maybe these questions have highlighted where you might need to develop or expand your awareness of necessary collaboration skills. Now that you've examined each dimension individually it's probably useful to take stock. So, finish by giving yourself an at-a-glance overview. Being able to take in all the elements in one overview can sometimes provoke new insights about useful next steps. Once you've added your scores, and as you step back, what strikes you?

Insecure		Confident
0	5	10
Rigid		Flexible
0	5	10
Has to be my way		Adapt to others
0	5	10
I want to get the credit		I don't care about the credit
0	5	10

Doesn't see benefits		Sees benefits
0	5	10

Focus on means as most important		Focus on means in service of ends
0	5	10

Win-lose		Win-win
0	5	10

Your Next Steps In Being a Collaborative Leader

Now that you have looked in the mirror and taken stock, how do you see yourself? What do you want to do? Do you still want to collaborate more effectively with others? Are you now ready to collaborate with others?

If you are ready (and brave enough), give the seven key questions from this chapter to three or four people who know you very well and with whom you have collaborated, and ask them to give you their impressions about your collaborative style and skills. To get 360 feedback, ask a range of people—perhaps a couple of colleagues, someone who reports to you or whom you guide, and your boss or someone who manages you.

Chapter 3

What Is a Collaborative Leader?

> Great leaders and followers are always engaged in a creative collaboration.
>
> **Warren Bennis, *On Becoming a Leader* (2003)**

It takes a great leader to facilitate collaborations. But being a collaborative leader is not about being nice or conciliatory. It is about pulling people together to tackle a challenge which is so big that it cannot be done alone.

The Collaboration That Prevented a Civil War

If there was ever a collaboration that changed the world, one that would certainly qualify for that status is the partnership between Nelson Mandela and F. W. de Klerk. In 1989, when they began their conversations, one man was the president of South Africa and the other was a prisoner. In fact, Nelson Mandela had been in prison for twenty-seven years in his fight against apartheid. In that year, de Klerk had become president and had the vision of a future in a post-apartheid South Africa.

On 2 February 1990 he "unbanded" the African National Congress (ANC), together with other liberation movements, released political prisoners, and suspended capital punishment. Then Mandela, after more than 10,000 days in prison and now 71 years old, walked free. That was one step in the collaboration. Many more would occur in the following years as together they made their joint vision a reality. Then, most amazingly, after only four years, Nelson Mandela would be voted as the new president in the first non-racial, democratic election. That was 27 April 1994.

How could all of this happen? How could a country torn apart by apartheid for half a century not end with a civil war? How could a new party coming to power not wreak revenge on their former persecutors? This powerful collaboration occurred because Mandela was larger than the unfair persecution, the lack of justice, the hatred, the contempt, or his need for revenge. In his 11 February speech, upon being freed, Mandela said:

> Today, the majority of South Africans, black and white, rec-ognize that apartheid has no future. It has to be ended by our own decisive mass action in order to build peace and security.
> …
> Mr. De Klerk has gone further than any other Nationalist president in taking real steps to normalise the situation. (Asmal et al., 2003, pp. 60–61)

And yet, fast forward past the years of Mandela's presidency and the beautiful collaboration that salvaged and began to democratize a nation, and we saw new levels of corruption in the government of President Jacob Zuma and a lack of the spirit of collaboration. This is a warning to us all: Even a historical collaboration of this magni-tude offers no guarantee of enduring if it is not picked up by others. Every generation has to reinvent the collaboration if it is to last. Every generation needs collaborative leaders who will continue that spirit.

After we began our collaboration on this book, Nelson Mandela died on 6 December 2013. After hearing about his death, de Klerk noted that Mandela did not just negotiate for his people. He also negotiated for the whites, arguing that their future had to be secure too. This is what prevented a civil war—a war that many expected and many were preparing for. Richard Stengel (2010) describes this as collaborating "with the enemy"—with those who had made Mandela's life and the lives of millions of black South Africans des-perate and poverty stricken.

A great example of this came in 1993 when South Africa was on the verge of civil war, when groups on the political extremes were arming for conflict and Mandela's political rival, Chris Hani, was murdered. Hani, the second most popular leader after Mandela, was a fiery speaker and committed communist. His assassination could have been the powder keg that set off a civil war. On the evening of his death, the person who spoke to the nation was not the president, F. W. de Klerk; it was Mandela.

Mandela addressed the nation and began by expressing and matching the hopes and fears of the South African people. He put their strongest feelings into words, validating their grief and anger on the one side and their shock on the other. In a calming voice and with authoritative presence, he set forth the collaborative vision:

> This is a watershed moment for all of us. Our decisions and actions will determine whether we use our pain, our grief, and our outrage to move forward to what is the only lasting solution for our country—an elected government of the people, by the people, and for the people. (Stengel, 2010, p. 49)

The collaboration that arose in South Africa, which saw a prisoner become a president, shows how even the most extreme positions and parties can work together. It is possible if there is vision, willingness, openness, dialogue, and, of course, collaborative leadership.

Making Collaboration Possible

Every collaboration ultimately operates as an intangible process and there has to be the right chemistry between people in order for them to work together effectively. But chemistry is one of those elusive things that you cannot see, hear, feel, smell, or taste. As a process, collaboration exemplifies how we relate, talk, get along, coordinate our schedules, and much more.

An effective collaboration is a dynamic, living, and interactive set of relationships. Accordingly, we should talk about collaborating as something we *do*. It requires qualities and actions from each person in the collaboration and, especially, it requires robust leaders. To begin with, it needs someone with a vision and a passion for that vision—someone willing to speak about, invite others to participate in, and inspire people to catch that vision.

The individual who leads an inspirational vision is a collaborative leader. She is proactive and focuses on inspiring that vision, not on status, prestige, position, or power. She prioritizes her activities so that she acts on what she envisions and doesn't talk it to death. Who is this kind of facilitative leader who leads out in creating collaboration? In a word, it is someone who has prepared herself by being ready and willing to step up and who is emotionally stable enough to create the collaboration. The collaborative leader can share leadership and participate as a good team player. This is as challenging as it is exciting.

The exciting part is easy and fun. It's exciting to catch a vision of the bigger game—what we can do together as a collaborative effort that we cannot do alone or apart. It's exciting to imagine the possibilities of bringing together multiple talented people, each sharing in the common goal and each contributing his or her part. It's exciting to be a part of a high performing team that creates a sense of belonging, a sense of "we" (as in "we are in this together"), and a sense that together we are more intelligent, effective, and powerful because of the collaboration.

Now for the challenging part. What is required to pull a team together in this way? What processes are involved? What does someone leading such an adventure have to do? Here are some of the important processes that frequently occur in a collaboration, any of which can make a massive difference to its success:

- Catching a common vision which speaks to a shared desire or problem.
- Communicating so each party understands each other with clarity and precision.
- Identifying the different talents and skills needed for actualizing the common vision.
- Coordinating the talents, skills, and schedule so that each person's contributions optimally contribute to the whole.
- Creating a culture or climate so that each individual feels safe to be open, to trust, to contribute, etc.
- Working out of the details for tapping in to the best that each person has to contribute.
- Developing ground rules for the collaboration and a way to use conflict positively to discover the best ideas, the best methods, and the best approaches.
- Working through the differences, conflicts, and frustrations of setbacks.
- Coordinating the tasks so that the collaboration is efficient and productive.

That's a lot! No wonder effective transformative collaborations do not "just happen." No wonder effective collaborations require an especially robust leader, someone who can bring people together and either coordinate the processes or facilitate the group to become a self-managing group.

Prerequisites For Collaborative Leadership

Perhaps the biggest and most important prerequisite for collaborative leadership is the ability to get your ego out of the way. If the collaboration is an adventure in making a vision real, then everyone in the collaboration has to put the vision first—and that means egos (personal agendas, individual glory, who gets the credit, etc.) must come second. This does not happen easily.

What is easy is for people to make the vision secondary to their own agendas and prestige, and to think about the vision with an eye on what they will get out of it. These can sabotage a collaborative vision and a collaborative group. So, first of all, the leader has to make his or her own ego subservient to the vision. What is needed for this is the belief that what we do together, we do in service of the greater good.

A great ball team does just that. Consider a team with superstars in it. If the superstar doesn't have a shot at the basket or goal post, he will give the opportunity to someone else. The success of the team comes first. If not, then the superstar might hog the openings and move the ball around until he gets the shot. What is on the person's mind is his own numbers and press, not the greater good of the team. So, although a team may contain one or more superstars, a team with good players—but no superstars—can often beat them. They do so because the team plays together and builds on each other's strengths, rather than competing against each other.

Helping Others Reduce Their Ego Filters

Here's another paradox: Collaboration happens *through* you but it is not *about* you. Yes, we collaborate because we have a vision and we want to achieve something, and yet it is about so much more than just "me." It is in this sense that we say collaborative leadership requires you to get your ego out of the way. But this is not sufficient on its own; it is common for others' egos to get in the way too. The signs of this problem include the following:

- They want certain things done their way.
- They want things done on their timetable.
- They want their positions and views to prevail.
- They are impatient and even intolerant with other views and ways of doing things.

- They are constantly pushing for recognition and status.
- They bad-mouth, gossip against, spread lies, and undermine the influence and power of those they consider to be their competitors.

Creating a Collaborative Culture

Getting our own ego out of our way, and helping others to do the same, marks the beginning of creating a collaborative culture. As a collaborative leader you need to be talking about collaboration and about what we are doing and can do together. This facilitates the vision and introduces the language of collaboration.

To lead a collaborative culture, the leader will want to positively reinforce every expression that is cooperative and collaborative. The reason for this is simple: What you reinforce will grow. If small acts of working together, thinking together, planning together, putting another person first, and celebrating his or her success are reinforced by giving attention to them, it sends a powerful message that collaboration *is* important and will be noticed and rewarded.

Similarly, when acts of wasteful competition occur and people expend energy fighting colleagues, particularly if such acts are not discouraged or even ignored, then individuals will get the message that this type of behavior is okay. Leadership is required at these times. Leaders need to be vigilant about the things that occur which undermine collaboration and address these as quickly as possible.

Stepping Up To Become a Collaborative Leader

If you are a lone wolf or lone ranger, are you a *real* leader? Is a leader a leader if he doesn't gather people around himself and empower them to feel that they are part of something bigger and better than all of them? This brings us back to one of the central themes in this book: Collaborative leadership is the next big challenge.

Anyone who thinks and calls himself a leader, but does not share, coordinate, cooperate, and create a sense of team, is actually self-deceived. That person is only a leader in his status or position, but not in the reality of leading people to work together. Does this mean that, as a leader, you always have to collaborate? The answer is no. In *Teams at the Top* (1998), Jon R. Katzenback notes that there are times when it is best to lead out as a leader in a single-leader mode rather than in a team-leader mode.

But how do you develop as a collaborative leader? What is involved in developing the skills of collaboration as a leader? In our opinion, stepping up to the challenge of collaborative leadership is the ultimate cutting-edge in leadership. This will involve seven key steps:

1. Setting the vision of collaborating for others and for yourself.
2. Recruiting people to join the collaboration.
3. Adding value to those who share your vision.
4. Communicating constantly to keep the vision and the mission alive.
5. Orchestrating people as collaborative partners of the vision.
6. Making yourself open and vulnerable to people.
7. Adding rich and robust meaning.

1. Setting the Vision of Collaborating For Others and For Yourself

Since vision drives big outcomes, start with a vision. What is yours? How robust is your vision? How exciting is it? If you are more excited about doing things to gain glory, recognition, praise, and so on, then it will be very hard to create a compelling vision of collaboration. This goes right to the heart of leadership. John Maxwell (2012) put it best when he said, "He that thinketh he leadeth, and hath no one following, is only taking a walk." To be a leader you have to win the minds and hearts of people. You have to attract them to a vision that captures their imagination. Are you doing that? Are you willing to learn how to do that?

For Steve Jobs, the inspiration he set at Apple was "to put a dent in the universe," so his employees all had the sense that they would be making something "insanely great." While Jobs lacked many of the personal and social skills needed to be a collaborative leader, his vision did indeed bring people together in collaborative projects.

How did Nelson Mandela acquire his collaborative vision? He grew up with it. It was part of the chieftaincy of his early life, as Richard Stengel describes in *Mandela's Way*:

The chiefly style of leadership was not about vaulting oneself to the front but about listening and achieving consensus.

The meetings of the royal court, which were like democratic town hall meetings, were the locus of leadership. All of the men from the village came, and anyone who wanted to speak could do so. It was the custom for the chief to listen to the views of his counselors and the community before uttering his own opinion. The king always stood up straight and proud, and when he spoke at the end of the meeting he would summarize the views that he had heard.

This is what Mandela means by *leading from behind*. … He listens, he summarizes, and then he seeks to mold opinion and steer people toward an action. … The African model of leadership is better expressed as *ubuntu*, the idea that people are empowered by other people, that we become our best selves through unselfish interaction with others. (2010, pp. 80–81)

2. Recruiting People To Join the Collaboration

Who will join you? Who do you want on the team? Who do you need on the team? Those collaborative leaders who do recruitment best look for two things in prospective team members: excellence in the development of skills and relational competency to work with others. Walt Disney did this. He had an eye for talent and so intentionally went out to recruit the talent that he needed. Do you have an eye on people, on their talents and skills? Do you invite these individuals into the collaboration?

> One of a leader's greatest challenges these days is getting people to actually talk to each other.
> **Richard Branson, *Like a Virgin* (2012)**

3. Adding Value To Those Who Share Your Vision

People follow a vision, so the leader should set out a vision that enables team members to recognize that there is something in it for them. What they should see is that the vision, and all of the effort that goes into actualizing it, will make their life better. It should also improve the quality of life for others. Leaders who believe that people stand in adoration of their intelligence, good looks, charm, and rhetorical skills want to be a cult leader, guru, or dictator, not a true leader. A leader who wants to be adored for her brilliance will not be able to function as a collaborative leader. Her ego will be in the way. It's about the leader, not the vision.

Here is a paradox: Leadership is not *about* the leader; it is *through* the person of the leader. This refers to the fact that leadership is not about the leader—it is about the shared vision. Yet leadership occurs through the vessel of the leader, as an exemplar of the vision, and through the leader's inspiration and work. The true leader leads by going first. She invests as much value as possible into the vision and into the team in order to make it happen. How does this settle with you? Are you adding significant value to those who raise their hands to say they want to be a part of where you're going and what you're doing? What are you investing in them? How often do you think about how you could add more value to them?

4. Communicating Constantly To Keep the Vision and the Mission Alive

The work of leadership is not over with the creation of the vision. Actually that's when the work begins. Next comes the effort of keeping the vision before people and letting them help to co-create the ongoing evolution of the vision as things change and develop. This work also includes gathering people together to find solutions to the obstacles that block the vision.

The vision you create as a leader will not endure in the minds and hearts of your team unless you are constantly refreshing it, providing new and different ways of expressing it, and getting people involved in moving toward it. It is never enough to state the vision and leave it at that. As a leader, your task is to make the vision come alive—to sing and dance in the minds of your team so that it stays meaningful and significant. Are you doing that? Do you know how to do that? Are you willing to learn how to do that?

5. Orchestrating People As Collaborative Partners of the Vision

From the activity of communicating constantly comes the leadership skill of involving people in practical ways that turn them into collaborative partners. This means sharing the vision-making process with them. This means bringing people into the inner circle and empowering them with decision-making powers. This means transferring responsibilities to them and trusting them to come through.

To become co-leaders of the vision, individuals will want to have a say and be consulted. True leaders do not create followers; they create more leaders. They groom others to become the next generation of leaders. How are you doing at that? Who are you grooming to be part of your leadership team? Who are you preparing to assume leadership powers and responsibilities?

Orchestrating involves management but this doesn't mean control. It means enabling people to discover their talent, place, contribution, and greatness. Orchestrating includes fostering the sense of being autonomous so that individuals can flourish. It's like a maestro who draws out the greatness in others and thereby makes the magic possible. Yes, orchestrating is planning, and yet it is more—it is meta-detailing the core processes for success. This does not constitute micro-managing or demanding perfection.

6. Making Yourself Open and Vulnerable To People

Leaders are not invincible statues made of stone; they are flesh and blood and suffer the same fallibilities of mind, emotion, speech, and behavior as the rest of us. A true leader leads out in being authentic, real, and down to earth. True leaders do not hide behind personas or masks. They come out from behind their personas and show their humanity. They are open, and even vulnerable, with others. They let people see their heart.

If this seems scary and frightening, you're right—it is. As a collaborative leader your challenge is to embrace it. When people know your heart and sense your passion for the vision, they will realize they can trust you. There is no hidden agenda and no secrets. As a leader you are upfront, straightforward, candid, transparent, and a truth-speaker. How are you doing with this? This may be at the very heart of how to be a collaborative leader—leading from your authenticity.

7. Adding Rich and Robust Meaning

Everyone should know the meaning of their work and contribution. Work that has meaning ceases to be work; it becomes a mission. When people contribute in a collaborative community, when they are regularly reminded of the meaningfulness of what they are doing and how it relates to the vision, they give much more fully of themselves—heart and mind.

Your Next Steps In Being a Collaborative Leader

Leadership is one thing; collaborative leadership is another. The traditional way of thinking about leaders is based on either military leadership or heroic leadership—two legitimate kinds of leadership but also two unique and unusual forms. Most work in organizations or business is not a military campaign against an enemy which has to be defeated. Nor is it a heroic act of saving something on the verge of death.

Instead, the kind of leadership most often needed in families, businesses, organizations, projects, and corporations is collaborative. This is leadership that pulls people together and brings out their best. It is not the leadership of a general who uses command and control as his methodology. It is the leadership of a caring visionary who thinks win-win and who communicates in a way that inspires, informs, and frames.

Use the following checklist to gauge your current capacity for collaborative leadership:

- I have a vision about a desired future or a problem that needs to be solved.
- I inspire people to share this vision in the ways that I communicate.
- I think win-win and operate from a position of mutual benefit.
- I know how to bring together diverse people with complementary skills to be part of a collaborative partnership.
- I have the administrative skills to coordinate the talents and skills of people on the project.
- I know how, and am able, to create a culture of collaboration.
- I am able to bring out the best in each person so that he or she feels able to contribute to the collaborative project.

- I have the necessary skills to coach or facilitate the team to work together through differences and conflicts.
- I am able to establish the ground rules of our collaboration and then graciously confront anyone who doesn't hold up his or her end.
- I am willing and able to co-lead with one or more other collaborative leaders.

Chapter 4

Challenges To Collaborative Leadership

9/11 was a failure of collaboration between FBI, Police, and CIA.

Morten Hansen, *Collaboration* **(2009)**

Trust is vital. People trust you when you don't play games with them, when you put everything on the table and speak honestly to them. Even if you aren't very articulate, your intellectual honesty comes through, and people recognize that and respond positively.

Warren Bennis, *On Becoming a Leader* **(2003)**

If collaborative leadership was easy, it would be occurring everywhere all of the time. It is not. It is challenging. Lots of things can prevent it, sabotage it, and make it go awry. Forewarned is forearmed, so it is helpful to know about the challenges that a budding collaborative leader will face. In this chapter we will describe some of the ways collaborations can go wrong, including deceptive pseudo-collaborations, barriers to collaboration, and collaborative crises.

Let Me Count the Ways—The Ways Collaborations Can Go Wrong

Collaborations go wrong more often than they go well—they are unsuccessful 50 percent of the time, sometimes 70 percent of the time.[1] So, what's the problem? Basically, anything that is corrosive of trust is a barrier to collaborating and will cause a collaboration to go wrong. Trust is the glue, so without it, collaboration means

---

1   In *Collaborative Leadership,* David Archer and Alex Cameron suggest that half of all alliances break down prematurely (2009, p. 125).

that you are risking lots of things—money, time, effort, reputation, and so on. In *The Collaborative Imperative* (2011, p. 121), Ron Ricci and Carl Wiese, assert: "Trust anchors every successful collaborative team … Articulate the team's purpose and establish upfront what you expect from each member."

A Failed Collaboration—The First Human Potential Movement

The Human Potential Movement (HPM) had its source in Abraham Maslow, and from him it spread like a virus. The idea of a psychology for human potential resonated with hundreds, and then thousands, and then hundreds of thousands of people. The movement began very slowly, with Maslow and Carl Rogers mapping out the healthy side of human nature and beginning to frame "human nature" in an entirely new way—that growth and development were natural, organic, and innate.

Maslow began in 1935 by modeling the characteristics, qualities, and beliefs of his two mentors, Max Wertheimer (a co-founder of Gestalt psychology) and Ruth Benedict (a co-founder of cultural anthropology). As a behaviorist, he had noticed that they were both very mature, healthy, "wonderful, wonderful" people. He also noted in his autobiography that he could not understand them—at least, not with the tools of psychology that were available to him at that time (i.e., behaviorism and psychoanalysis). This initiated his exploration. He began a book, *Good Humans Studies*, and afterwards he went on to develop humanistic (or self-actualization) psychology.

He spent the next three decades studying the lives and characteristics of thousands of people who demonstrated some of the same self-actualizing qualities. By 1943 he had created the hierarchy of needs model, but he spent another thirteen years in research before he wrote his classic work, *Motivation and Personality* (1954). With that book the HPM took off internationally.

Aldous Huxley began talking about the need for a movement for human potential in his lectures. So did Rollo May, Roberto Assagioli, and dozens of others. In a similar manner, they wrote about the possibilities of human potential. As they did so, Maslow welcomed each and every one of them into the movement. He did this by naming them, embracing them, and calling them "colleagues" (Maslow's inclusive spirit is readily observable in his writings). Then, as things developed, he invited his new colleagues to conferences, panels, and other forums to give them an opportunity for their voice and contribution to be heard—for example, a number of anthologies were published, many of which were edited by Maslow.

In these and many other ways, Maslow became a collaborator and demonstrated the skills of collaboration. But collaboration must be mutual, and this is where the HPM failed. While Maslow and his students (Everett Shostrom, James Bugental, Colin Wilson, etc.) were definitely collaborative in their communications and actions, very few of those who were invited in were similarly collaborative.

It is clear from several of the histories written about Esalen that what went on at the very place which was designed to be the think-tank of the HPM was anything but collaborative. In his biography of Esalen, Jeffrey Kripal (2007) describes the atmosphere as one of war. The question was, who would plant their flag and try to make HPM theirs? Would it be Fritz Perls? He was Maslow's most competitive, even combative, rival. Would it be Will Schutz? He wrote *Joy* in 1967 and put HPM on the map in the United States. He later claimed to be the "Emperor of Esalen" and the founder of HPM! Even Carl Rogers, after Maslow's death, claimed to be the sole founder of HPM.

Several years ago, I (LMH) detailed all of this in an article titled, "How to Kill a Movement."[2] The point of the article was to say that collaboration has to be mutual. There has to be give and take and a deep collegial attitude. There has to be a generous spirit and an attitude of recognizing others. If not, then any group that results from the single leader's vision and values will only last as long as that leader and his or her influence lasts. This was the case with the first HPM.

An Asymmetrical Collaboration

A collaboration that I (LMH) was involved in for five years, and which worked at first and then went wrong, was established with an event organizer. She contacted me due to my reputation in the field of NLP as a trainer and author and invited me to her country. That was a win for me: I wanted to launch my work in that country. It was

---

2   I (LMH) studied and restudied the works of Abraham Maslow, Carl Rogers, and most of the other leaders of the first Human Potential Movement. I did so to fully understand the models of self-actualization whereby people can identify and unleash their potential and become "fully functioning persons" (Rogers, 1961).

also a win for her: She needed an internationally known trainer with a good reputation.

I was her vision of this person. However, at the time, I didn't explore her vision of the collaboration. Big mistake. What we did discuss was the *how* of working together and the mechanics, but not the *why*. Had we done so we would have talked about a shared vision, and I would have discovered from the beginning that we had two very different visions of what each of us wanted to achieve.

So, without due diligence, we engaged in a collaboration which worked reasonably well for a few years. However, during that time there were several occasions when it became obvious to both of us that we operated from very different values and visions. For her it was all about business, so the only measurement of success was financial. For me, I had a vision of creating a more positive reputation for NLP, of building an enduring community, of adding more value to what we offered, and of demonstrating the quality and kind of leadership that would change the field over the coming decades.

The collaboration broke down when it became obvious that we had different ideas about what each of us thought should be our next level of development. For her it was to introduce a "hard sales" approach to the training. For me it was to introduce support practice groups. The end was in sight, but we "needed" each other for another year of trainings, which we duly undertook. But during that time the spirit of collaboration was gone. While we managed to put on a friendly face publicly, behind the scenes there was a mutual disrespect of each other's values and a sense that the other lived in an alien world.

What went wrong? At some level, what we had was only an instrumental collaborative relationship, but we didn't know it (well, I didn't know it). We had not spent sufficient time getting to know each other as individuals who would be collaborating. We had focused entirely on practical business matters. For my part, I had assumed it was a visionary collaborative relationship, but I had not checked this out sufficiently with her. I supposed that since she had chosen me, and we were in the same field, then we would share the same vision. So, in the last days, even though we had agreed to share our mutual assets and resources, she refused to share the database we had co-created. Despite never having done anything to undermine her trust, she refused to accept my word that I would not compete with her by offering the same (or even a similar) product.

I made several learnings from this experience. The first learning was: How a collaboration begins makes a difference. Looking back,

I realize that the collaboration was time limited from the start because it did not have a solid enough foundation for the long term. I also discovered that we had entered the collaboration too lightly, too quickly, and without sufficient common vision about what we were collaborating to do. For a short-term ad hoc collaboration it worked fine; but it was not enough for a long-term visionary collaboration. It was not even a pseudo-collaboration (see below and Chapter 17); it was purely an instrumental relationship.

When you collaborate, make sure you explore the following points with your team:

- How are we beginning this collaboration?
- What are our shared visions and values as we begin?
- Is anyone on the rebound or simply trying to replace a former partner?
- Do we want to create a short-term or long-term collaboration?

The challenge is not merely to create more collaborations; it is to create the *right* collaboration. Just because there is an opportunity to collaborate does not mean you should do so. After all, collaboration itself is not a panacea or the best solution for all circumstances. The right collaboration will be appropriate to the context, individuals, values, vision, timing, resources, and so on.

Pseudo-Collaborations

Here's another challenge: Not everything called collaboration actually is a collaboration. You may have a collaboration and it may not be authentic. In some way or another it is fake. It's a pseudo-collaboration. What is it about these interactions that make them a pseudo-collaboration? How can people attempt to cooperate but not create the real thing?

Here are some of the factors that can mark a pseudo-collaboration:

- *Talk of collaboration*: Using the linguistics of collaboration so that your descriptions of interacting with others sound like collaboration, but in reality it is just talk. It may even be exciting and inspirational talk, but in the end nothing actually happens. It is talking the talk but not walking the walk.
- *Consensus*: Seeking to reduce the vision, the standards, and the

quality of an adventure with others so that we can get a consensus from everyone in the group. This is consensus, not genuine collaboration.

- *Networking*: Mixing and mingling with groups of people, and being seen and known by lots of people, is networking, not collaborating.
- *A single-leader group*: Leading a group to achieve some goal or outcome and calling it a collaboration. This is a pseudo-collaboration, not a collaboration.
- *Making a proposal*: Speaking up to make a proposal to an individual or a group, and then assuming that offering to take on a project is the same thing as a collaboration.
- *Delegation*: Getting people to do what you want by telling them, delegating to them, etc.
- *Cooperation*: Cooperation is not the same as collaboration even though the literal definitions have a similar root. Nick LeForce distinguishes these in the following way:

> Cooperation emphasizes getting along with others and working well with them. You typically cooperate for mutual gain. ... Collaboration also implies an active contribution by each party. You can cooperate with others without collaborating with them. In order to truly collaborate, you must invest yourself and actively seek to meet your own needs and those of others simultaneously. Collaboration requires a combination of healthy assertion and healthy cooperation. (2009, pp. 11–12)
>
> Collaboration is a step beyond cooperation and capitalizes on all three perceptual positions. (2009, p. 91).[3]

Barriers To Collaboration

What could stop you from effectively collaborating? Given that collaboration is a synthesis between self and other, between our skills of personal development (or self-development) and the development

---

3   In *Co-Creation: How to Collaborate for Results* (2009), Nick LeForce details the differences between the three NLP perceptual positions: the first person is "I" and sees things from the self; the second person steps into the other and can see, hear, and feel what the other person is experiencing—this is the empathetic perspective ("you"); and the third person is "we," as it sees the larger system that we are in.

of social skills, there are many barriers on each of these axes.

Here is a list of barriers on the self-development axis:

- Immaturity
- Fear
- Individualism
- Egotism/arrogance
- Self-absorption
- Lone star
- Power hungry
- Defensiveness

Here is a list of barriers on the social development axis:

- Socially undeveloped
- Scarcity
- Envy
- Resentment
- Hidden agenda(s)
- Social butterfly
- Social selfishness
- Lack of a role model

Where are you on the continuum from self-development to social development?

Self-development   Social development

Neurological Collaboration

Before concluding this chapter, we would like to stress that while collaboration may require effort—in fact, a lot of effort and work—collaboration is also a natural process. It is natural for one simple reason: because we are neurologically wired to collaborate.

In a world where resources are limited, the best strategy for survival might be to selfishly compete for the maximum resource that can be obtained by one individual. This is a description of Darwin's survival of the species where individual organisms compete to protect the reproduction of their own genes. However, some animal species, including humans, have developed neurological mechanisms that overcome this tendency, and which instead promote cooperation and collaboration (Rilling et al., 2002). In these species, a good turn or favor dispensed by one member of the species is often reciprocated by another, leading to a bond of trust. Additionally, when we receive a favor from someone, we are more likely to dispense a favor to someone else. This willingness to help is a form of altruism which helps to protect a larger number of individuals within a group. Working together has also been shown to improve sourcing of information, reasoning, and fairer allocation of resources.

There has been considerable research into the brain networks that drive this behavior. Each of these benefits depends on the free sharing of information between individuals—an important factor in collaboration. Since reciprocal altruism is so scarce in the animal kingdom, there must be specific conditions in which this arises. Over the course of our development, the ability to respond to and understand the behavior of others has arisen in stages. Three developmental stages have been recognized:

1. Affective arousal—there must be constant interaction between individuals across the lifespan.
2. Empathic concern—there has to be a mechanism to inhibit the tendency to act selfishly.
3. Empathic understanding—individuals must be able to identify members of their group(s) who do reciprocate and those who do not.

Darwin (1871) noted that:

[Sympathy] will have been increased through natural selection; for those communities, which included the greatest number of the most sympathetic members, would flourish best, and rear the greatest number of offspring. (Vol. I, p. 82)

The first stage in the evolution of empathy is *affective arousal*. This comes from an ability to detect and respond to our own emotional signals. It has been suggested that certain emotions have evolved to signal the need for changes in behavioral patterns. We can assign them to two broad categories. First, there are those emotions that signal approach and which serve to increase the behavior. These are positive emotions including joy, happiness, fulfillment, and compassion, and negative emotions such as anger. Second, there are emotions that signal avoidance and serve to decrease the behavior. These are negative emotions such as disgust, fear, sadness, guilt, and embarrassment.

The second stage is *empathic concern*. This is thought to have evolved partially in response to the development of the placenta in mammals and to the protracted development of offspring after birth, giving rise to extended parenting behaviors. Parenting behavior depends on the ability to determine emotions in others, especially hunger, pain, distress, and fear, an ability which appears early in mammalian evolution. This effect has been termed "emotional contagion" and is found in all mammalian species. Emotional contagion occurs when the vocal, facial, and gestural cues of one individual generate a similar state in another individual.

Emotional contagion is related to the release of oxytocin and vasopressin which both increase empathy by the carer and decrease fear and anxiety in the cared for, thus improving the welfare of the person being cared for. It has been found to cause changes in activity in the amygdala (it reduces social threat) and the prefrontal cortex (where it regulates emotional responses). Oxytocin has also been found to directly increase dopamine release, therefore providing a strong reward for caregiving behavior. It is this mechanism that is responsible for the choice to inhibit the tendency to act selfishly. The social reward that is gained from caring behaviors is sufficient to overcome the desire to act selfishly in many situations.

The third stage of development is *empathic understanding*. This more advanced form of empathy depends on the development of self-awareness which increases the capacity for empathy in two major ways: it allows us to determine and follow social norms based on the feedback that we receive from others, and it allows us to hypothesize about the emotional states of others in relation to our emotional state. Self-awareness is thought to develop over the second and third years of life. Being able to differentiate self and others is important in that it increases our ability to reflect on the thoughts, intentions, and emotions of others, hence increasing our ability to hypothesize about their potential actions. This is known as theory of mind.

The ability to recognize those who reciprocate and those who don't appears to be driven by a combination of oxytocin and theory of mind. While oxytocin has been demonstrated to increase trust in some situations it does not always improve social relations. It can also cause us to protect ourselves more from people who we do not consider to be part of our "group." Thus, oxytocin increases trust between members of a group, but decreases trust and can drive protective behaviors against people who are not group members. Theory of mind enables us to model the potential behaviors and intentions of others, allowing us to determine whether we consider them part of our group (and likely to help us) or a member of an out-group and therefore less trustworthy.

One of the more recent breakthroughs in neuroscience specifically demonstrates our social connection. The discovery of mirror neurons in 1992 has provided a neurological basis for learning through imitation. One theory suggests that what our mirror neurons do is give us the ability to quickly see and hear people—experiences on the outside—and then mirror the same on the inside. This is the basis of modeling response patterns that we see and hear in others.

The research suggests that humans are fundamentally social beings—that this is our natural social condition. Alfred Korzybski (1933) said that human beings are "time-binding creatures."[4] This refers to the way in which the learning we develop at one point in time can be represented in our neural activity, so that we make it our own. We do this through another type of collaboration—using common representational systems such as the symbols which form language. So, what Aristotle or Einstein or Bill Gates learned can be absorbed for use by others via common representations, including language.

In *The Fatal Conceit* (1988), economist and philosopher F. A. Hayek suggests that we are wired for cooperation:

These genetically inherited instincts served to steer the cooperation of the members of the troop, a cooperation that was

---

4   Korzybski said that plants are chemical-binders inasmuch as they bind the chemicals in the soil and elements in the air into themselves and thereby live and grow. Animals are space-binders in that they move about to obtain the nutrients needed for life. Humans do these things too and yet transcend them as they are also time-binders. They bind into themselves what was learned and developed in previous times by other humans. They take it in using the mechanisms of symbolism and language.

a narrowly circumscribed interaction of fellows known to and trusted by one another. … These modes of coordination depended decisively on instincts of solidarity and altruism— instincts applying to the members of one's own group but not to others. (pp. 11–12)

Differences among individuals increase the power of the collaborating group beyond the sum of individual efforts. Synergetic collaboration brings into play distinctive talents that would have been left unused had their possessors been forced to strive alone for sustenance. Civilization is based on human development in its richest diversity. The increasing intelligence shown by man is due not so much to increases in the several knowledge of individuals but to procedures for combining different and scattered information which, in turn, generate order and enhance productivity. (p. 80)

Your Next Steps In Being a Collaborative Leader

Knowing that there are and will be challenges when collaborating gives you a valuable heads-up, so that you can be more mindful of the potential pitfalls. Are you now alert to these challenges? How will you use this information as an early warning system? Ultimately, collaborating requires trust in others, the development of trust, a culture where trust can grow, and the call for trustworthiness. How trusting are you?

Part II

Collaborative Leadership— The How To

Chapter 5

The Collaborative Pathway

How Do We Get There?

If we are interconnected and the world is interconnected, the only way for the world to work is to have a set of common values. We have no option but to work together.

Tony Blair, former Prime Minister of the UK

Collaboration will be the critical business competency of the Internet age. It won't be the ability to compete, but the ability to lovingly cooperate that will determine success.

James M. Kouzes

Once a leader or a leadership team issues an invitation to collaborate, and people begin to entertain the possibility of a collaboration, the journey begins. You are now on a pathway—the collaborative pathway to create something together that exceeds what any one person could do alone or apart.

What is this journey, and how do we get to engage in a collaborative enterprise? What can you expect when you launch out on this adventure? How does it begin, develop, reach maturity, and end? What is the path of the collaboration? What are the steps and stages along the way? Can you reach your goal? All of these strategic questions are about the collaboration pathway—our focus in this chapter.

The ten key steps and stages which are typically involved in any successful collaborative process are:

1. A problem is encountered or a vision is imagined.
2. An invitation is presented.
3. A solution is explored, brainstormed, and discovered.
4. A challenge and commitment is accepted.
5. A strategy is agreed upon for the project.
6. The innovative solution is rolled out.
7. Ongoing problems and interferences arise and are dealt with.

8. The outcome is attained (the problem is solved or the objective is reached).
9. The collaboration success is celebrated.
10. The end is confirmed.

We're going to explore each of these steps in this chapter. Before we do, though, we want to introduce you to the prisoner's dilemma because it's a useful reminder of the kind of tensions that often need to be addressed to successfully collaborate.

The Prisoner's Dilemma

The prisoner's dilemma was a game set up originally to explore the inter-relationship between the twin drives of competing to get the best option and cooperation to create a win-win context with others. How do we create within ourselves an integration between these driving forces which seem to pull us in opposite directions? On the one hand there is the opportunity for cooperation or mutual gain, and on the other hand there is an enticement to compete which might mean a greater gain at another's expense.

Imagine this situation: two lawbreakers are arrested and questioned separately. If each person remains silent both of them are acquitted—a win for both. However, if one turns "state's evidence" (blames the other) he is lightly punished, while his accomplice gets a heavy sentence. However, neither prisoner knows what the other will do.

	Prisoner B cooperates	Prisoner B defects
Prisoner A cooperates	Each serves one month	Prisoner A serves three months Prisoner B goes free
Prisoner A defects	Prisoner A goes free Prisoner B serves three months	Each serves two months

If we give a value to each choice in this scenario, then we have the following:

- If both cooperate by remaining silent they each get three points as a reward for cooperating.
- If both defect by telling on the other they each get one point as a punishment for not joining forces.
- If one defects and the other cooperates, then the defector gets five points for competing and the trusting cooperator gets zero points for being a sucker.

Individual self-interest and collective well-being collide head-on in the prisoner's dilemma. Its diabolical simplicity has given rise to literally thousands of scientific experiments and papers to discover what is the best strategy, cooperate or defect?

What is seductive is that the biggest gain occurs by defecting when the other is cooperating. This is always the best option for a single person. The trouble is that the other player will probably be thinking along the same lines. If that happens, then both end up with only one point, which is the worst result for both—two points less than if they both cooperated.

This is not just a strange set-up for torturing university students. In most social contexts, competition and cooperation are present to varying degrees and combinations. Two fundamental human motives are present in the dilemma: greed for gain through exploiting others and fear of loss through being exploited. Each motive alone is destructive. Together they create a "let others do it" society in which not a single other ever does.

	He cooperates	He competes
I cooperate	Good neighbors	Exploited
I compete	Exploited	Mutual damage

So what has the research shown? Several things. First, people who take the competitor position wrongly assume that all their opponents are also competitors, even when they play as cooperators. It has been shown that cooperators are far more accurate in recognizing what their opponents are doing, whether competing or cooperating.

Psychologist Morton Deutsch, who has studied altruism and cooperation, suggests:

> Competitive and cooperative processes tend to be self-confirming so that the experience of cooperation will induce a benign spiral of increasing cooperation, while competition will induce a vicious spiral of intensifying competition. (1973, p. 31)

So what is best? Is winning the main thing? Is it the only thing to live for? Or is the dominant strategy that it is best for everyone to cooperate? The bottom line is that in the long term, the most productive and profitable strategy is to start from the cooperative position, but to stay alert to what happens and shift accordingly if necessary. So when the opponent competes, compete. When you see that your opponent is cooperating, go back to cooperating. These are the learnings that arise from the prisoner's dilemma.

With this sobering perspective in mind, let's now walk through the ten steps.

1. A Problem (Or Need) Is Encountered Or a Vision Is Imagined

Collaboration often begins with a need, desire, problem, or vision. Someone sees or senses an issue that needs to be dealt with or solved, or sees or senses the possibility of a desired vision. From this encounter arises the energy for the engine of collaboration. This is especially true when the need or desire is too big for one person to tackle single-handed.

Michael's Story

After entering the sphere of NLP, I began noticing several problems in the field. The problems were mostly ethical and arose from misusing the models and from not walking the talk. So I started talking about the abuses I was seeing—I really disliked it when I saw someone manipulating others with the powerful communication tools of

NLP. And I found it disturbing when I saw others behaving in ways incongruent with what they were teaching. For me it was unethical and unprofessional. Eventually, I collaborated with three other trainers and we wrote about it in an article called, "Dealing with the Downside of NLP," which was the first paper to offer a critique on this issue. That was in 1993.

A few years later, in 1996, I encountered more instances of the problem. Richard Bandler, one of the co-founders of NLP, had decided to sue "the field of NLP" in the United States. He filed a $90 million lawsuit claiming to hold the trademark and therefore "own" the discipline. In the process he disqualified almost every trainer. That's when I entered into a collaboration with Bob Bodenhamer to do something about it.

As licensed NLP Trainers we knew that if the lawsuit succeeded, we would not be able to train people in NLP, as we had done for years. As we talked about this problem, as well as the other issues we saw in our field, we caught the vision of something we could do to tackle it. Our vision was to formulate a community within NLP that was dedicated to an ethical approach—one that placed applying the principles and practices of NLP to oneself as foundational. Using the terminology of Alfred Korzybski in *Science and Sanity* (1933), we named it "Neuro-Semantics."

As part of the collaboration, Bob decided to create a website and asked me to write a vision statement that he could display on the site. I quickly put into words the vision we had discussed and had come to believe in for our field:

Our vision is to take NLP to a higher level professionally and ethically. It is to *live* out the NLP premises of operating from a state of abundance, being collaborative, giving credit to sources, and always treating people with dignity and honor.

It was that simple. Within a few days, someone called and asked what was required to join "The Society of Neuro-Semantics." We didn't know the answer. Incredibly, we had not thought that far in advance! By the end of the week, seven more wanted to join. Today, there are thousands of trainers, coaches, and members of the International Society of Neuro-Semantics in forty-four countries.

Ian's Story

Back in 1988, I founded International Teaching Seminars so that I could make available some of the exciting new approaches to successful personal and organizational change management which I was involved in helping to develop. Back then, it seemed to me that we were really making headway in finding out what actually worked. However, what we didn't have was the neurological explanation for why what my colleagues and I were doing worked. This was a source of ongoing fascination and frustration for me.

For many years, I continued to collaborate with colleagues to develop and promote new applications for the NLP tools we had found so impactful. Only in the last few years has it been possible for me to realize my dream of achieving a real interface between neuroscience and NLP.

I spent many years talking to neuroscientists—I was looking for one or more who were interested in change technologies and had the scientific credentials to speak to what worked and why. Eventually I met Patricia Riddle who had thirty years of research experience and, most unusually, had completed NLP Practitioner training. As she tells the story, she was dragged into it screaming, but then found it really interesting. She was nonplussed by how her trainers would demonstrate a technique with success and then say, "But neuroscience doesn't accept this." She would seek to correct this impression by saying, "As a neuroscientist this makes perfect sense, and I can tell you why." However, her trainers did not pursue the matter.

When she first told me this story I was astonished. Here was what I'd been looking for! The timing was fortuitous. Patricia was contemplating what her official designation as a professor of neuroscience should be. I asked her what mattered to her most and she said applying neuroscience. So it was that she became a Professor of Applied Neuroscience.

When we agreed to collaborate, our big picture vision was, first, to bring what neuroscience can offer to the world and, second, to use neuroscience to explain why certain extant interventions work. We began by adding a neuroscience component to the NLP Practitioner training I delivered (Patricia comes in on the final morning of each module and provides a neuroscience review of the previous two days' training). This we designed together. It gave us an opportunity to work together in public and develop a common language.

We both found this incredibly rewarding. It encouraged us to go further. Our next project was to co-create a part-time program designed to distil current neuroscience research and show how to apply it. The result was the Certificate in Applied Neuroscience which has now become an annual program.

If we unpack this initiative, the problem was that years of neuro-science research seemed "stuck in the lab"—in the sense that laypeople were either unaware of or not clear how to make use of what had been learned. (Many people's understanding of the brain is somewhere between thirty to forty years out of date. I cannot think of another discipline where this is true.)

We began to explore a variety of solutions, settled on one—a certified program—which would be a good place to start, agreed a strategy, and rolled out the solution. For us, the main problem has been doing all this while fulfilling our other professional responsibil-ities. Doing it once, however, does not achieve the outcome of making what is available widely known. Hence our continued com-mitment to doing it, plus the suite of new initiatives that have grown out of this. There has been much to celebrate but, for us, the collab-oration journey continues.

2. An Invitation Is Presented

The invitation is a request to solve a problem or fulfill a vision. Usually the invitation begins when someone thinks aloud in the presence of one or more people. Later, the invitation becomes more formal and is presented as a proposal to do something together. Invitations are often of the form, "Someone ought to do something about this!"

The vision that I (LMH) created for Neuro-Semantics grew out of a dialogue with perhaps a dozen people about the idea of "taking NLP to a higher level." As the vision was formulated, I initially invited four individuals who shared the same idea to join me, from which emerged the first Society of Neuro-Semantics. Soon thereaf-ter we invited two others, but they turned down the invitation to be a part of the pioneering group. While they broadly agreed with the vision, they felt it was too risky for their reputations to publicly say that they felt NLP had experienced a lot of bad press and needed to be reformed.

In the case of my (Ian) collaboration with Patricia, my curiosity led me to make the invitation. This began the exploration which became a series of trainings in an interdisciplinary area which we both loved.

3. A Solution Is Explored, Brainstormed, and Discovered

From the need or desire comes the exploration, the brainstorming, and eventually the discovery of solutions. The solution could be a product, service, information, or experience. From the collaboration of several or many minds and conversations, ideas emerge as people consider the possibilities of what they can do to address the original stimulus for the collaboration.

Finding and/or creating a solution lies at the very heart of a collaboration. Research has demonstrated that if the collaboration is organized around a focused objective, groups can be more creative and produce a higher quality of creativity than individuals can alone. As the saying goes, "All of us are smarter than any one of us."

The solution that I (LMH) created with Bob Bodenhamer, and then many others, first became a movement, then a few years later Neuro-Semantics became a community and eventually an international organization. At first, the solution was to be the change and experience we talked about and described. For us, this meant putting "apply to self" into the very vision and formula of Neuro-Semantics. Part of the answer was also the value of letting things evolve. This was formulated in the statement, "We continuously invent it as we go," which put constant improvement and ongoing evolution at the core of the community.

4. A Challenge and Commitment Is Accepted

Creating a solution is not the end; it is actually just the beginning of a collaboration. After a workable, actionable solution has been created comes the hard part of taking on the challenge of applying the solution. This means getting buy-in to the change or project. The mental collaboration that generates good ideas, even great ideas, will come to nothing if there isn't leadership. It is leadership which takes a great idea and transforms it into a vision, and then invites buy-in from those who could possibly turn it into reality.

I (LMH) thought that it was a great idea to create a whole community of people living the values of NLP—ethical, professional, ecological, good communicators, working through conflicts, sharing resources, giving credit where credit belongs, collaborating as partners, and so on. I loved the idea and I believed that many others would love the idea as well. I also knew that it would be challenging for some people to make the required changes in order to practice and live out that idea. That would be a very different matter indeed. So, over the years, the "experiment" of Neuro-Semantics underwent numerous transformations. This was true of the leadership team that we put together. It has also been true of all the institutes we have launched in two dozen countries around the world. We continue to invent things as we go.

In 2010, while in South Africa, I set out a problem and a vision to our Meta-Coaches in the Neuro-Semantic community: "How many of you have said about NLP, 'They ought to teach this stuff to kids?' How many of you have wondered, 'Why don't they teach this material in schools?'" Everybody acknowledged that they had thought this and most affirmed that they had actually said this at one time or another. "So let's do it!" I proposed. "Let's take the basic materials of NLP and meta-states and let's create a daily lesson plan for teachers and grade-age appropriate workbooks for children." And that's precisely what we did.

Using the adult materials for six days of training (forty-eight hours), which introduced the fundamentals of the NLP Communication Model and the Meta-States Model as applied to personal mastery, forty Meta-Coaches wrote twelve grades of workbook. Each grade-age appropriate workbook has forty lessons, one for each of the forty weeks of a school year, and each one designed for a one-hour lesson. The theme of all of the materials is self-leadership.

While it may sound simple, this was a major project. First, a leadership team of seven people plotted out the forty lessons with the themes for each level, and then gathered two to four people to do the actual design and writing for each of the twelve grades. The adult manuals are 150 pages long and so are each of the twelve grades. In the meantime, a company in South Africa took the lead, AMKA Products, under the guidance of CEO Nizam Kalla, who identified a local school in Johannesburg to run the program throughout their school year as our prototype.

Altogether, the challenge and commitment to complete the project took approximately two and a half years. Today we are making the materials available to any school in the world. This has led to other groups in our community translating the materials into Spanish, Norwegian, Chinese, and Portuguese.

5. A Strategy Is Agreed Upon For the Project

From leadership vision and values to the management of the specific processes, a strategy has to be developed. This refers to generating a strategic way to organize, budget, structure, and problem-solve so that the collaboration can move forward. The collaboration now comes down to the management of the day-to-day tasks that have to be done to make the solution successful.

In my case (LMH), this meant doing something that I really did not want to do and still do not think I'm very good at. It meant shifting from the role of setting the vision and inspiring it, which I'm experienced at and enjoy, to administrating it. It meant creating, with Bob Bodenhamer, the first website, setting up and monitoring e-groups, getting non-profit status with the Internal Revenue Service, trademarking and registering Neuro-Semantics, setting up a bank account, instituting processes for the leadership team to meet and make decisions, recording decisions and plans, and lots of other things.

These types of administrative tasks are not my forte. But if the vision was to see the light of day, I knew that it had to be done. In the early years, I often let important things slip that I should have attended to with more focus. Yet those mistakes, and my lack of attention to such details, taught me how to deal with administrative responsibilities and learn the skill of meta-detailing. This is the skill of holding the larger perspective (the meta-frame of reference) and simultaneously identifying the specific details that make it actual.

6. The Innovative Solution Is Rolled Out

The strategy for managing the solution is to take the innovative solution that has arisen from the collaboration and then to roll it out. What is rolled out as the implementation is the actual day-to-day activities that make the creative solution real. This is where the vision is realized in the lives of those who make up the collaboration.

My (LMH) collaborative project in Neuro-Semantics meant rolling out the meeting and decision-making processes of the leadership team and determining how the institutes would operate as self-managing units with their own local leadership teams to support and promote Neuro-Semantics in different countries. In 2007, we rolled out a new initiative, the "New Human Potential Movement," in a series of workshops, seminars, and announcements. In 2009, we introduced a set of "Professional Tracks in Neuro-Semantics," which would be a new way for trainers to sell their training. In 2010, we decided to launch a biennial international conference, which we staged first in Colorado in 2011 and then in Kuala Lumpur, Malaysia in 2013.

7. Ongoing Problems and Interferences Arise and Are Dealt With

The execution stage of implementing and rolling out the solution to a need or desire begins a whole series of problem-solving challenges. Everything that arises as a block or interference to the success of the collaboration requires additional solutions, resources, energy, money, and time. But for the collaboration to succeed, this is just an inevitable stage of the process. It is the phase of adjusting the creative solution to the reality of the context where the innovation occurs.

To my (LMH) dismay (well, at least at first), I discovered that another solution had to be implemented if we were to realize our vision of living the ethical and professional standards, so I created the "Conflict Resolution Process." This is an agreement which every licensed trainer and Meta-Coach signs as part of their licensure. It addresses how we will work through conflicts. In it, we commit ourselves to working through a structured process wherein we will confront and deal with conflicts that could divide us. Today this is built in to the licensing process, as well as the information details about what it means to be a licensed trainer or coach under the International Society of Neuro-Semantics. As people might not follow through on this commitment to work things out if they had been found to be involved in fraudulent practices, we created a way to highlight this and warn others about them.

Another problem that we discovered and have addressed in Neuro-Semantics stems from our goal for continuous improvement. We continually update the training manuals and we revisit our practices and decisions on a regular basis. My own commitment is to update each training manual every year and so we have incorporated the practice of naming the edition (i.e., edition 8, 9, 10). This creates additional problems for everybody when translating the text into Spanish, Chinese, Portuguese, French, and so on, and yet it is necessary if we are to not solidify things so they become written in stone.

8. The Outcome Is Attained (the Problem Is Solved Or the Objective Is Reached)

Through applying and executing ongoing improvement processes, the original goal of the collaboration should succeed. The outcome is attained, which marks the achievement of the collaboration.

For example, for over two years we had forty Meta-Coaches working to create the Self-Leadership School Project. It was completed in December 2012 and put on the website for trainers and coaches. This project is a set of forty lesson guides for schoolchildren for one hour once a week. So, in every grade (from grades 1 to 12), the children learn the patterns of NLP and meta-states around the theme of self-leadership. Once a week, every week, at their grade-age level, they learn the patterns for taking charge of their own minds, emotions, and their responses. Once the project was completed, it was released to more than 2,000 trainers and coaches to make available in any school system.

9. The Collaboration Success Is Celebrated

If the collaboration is time limited or a one-off event (e.g., to solve a problem or fulfill a desired outcome), then the collaboration will end upon completion. In that case, a natural stage of the process is to celebrate your success and bring closure to the collaborative partnership. If the collaboration requires an ongoing and continuous implementation, then the celebrations will take place at chosen milestones.

Here, again, I (LMH) realized a weakness in myself as a leader. My own personal mental program about "celebration" is that the achievement of an outcome is itself the celebration. I hardly need do anything else except just to notice and appreciate. However, over the years I've had enough feedback to realize that this is not sufficient for most people. I know this because lots of people have commented on it, so I've been learning.

One everyday piece of celebration is an innovation that we put into all of our competency-based trainings—the morning celebration. In the longer trainings (those that last eight to fifteen days), we create a Celebrate Board on which people can place Post-it notes of acknowledgments of their learnings, discoveries, breakthroughs, and so on. Each morning, we ask those on the assist team who are most skilled at leading a celebration to read and acknowledge the achievements. We end those training sessions with a formal ceremony of celebration, usually taking two full hours for that, and providing wine and finger food for the party that follows.

10. The End Is Confirmed

How will you recognize the completion of a collaboration? Will you take time to do or say something that will honor the adventure and bring the experience to a good close? For a time-limited collaboration, the ending should be treated with as much importance and significance as the beginning. Reviewing the process, recognizing what worked well—and learning from what didn't—are an important part of the experience, so the collaboration will be remembered fondly and used as a resource for future collaborations.

In 2010, I (LMH) invited Shelle Rose Charvet to work with me in creating the very first collaboration book in the field of NLP, *Innovations in NLP*. We put out a call to collect new patterns, models, and products in the field of NLP. Over a six month period, we collaborated with twenty-four contributors who wrote seventeen chapters about new models, patterns, and applications. Then, in November 2011, at the NLP Conference in London, we held a book launch, with a dozen of the authors who had contributed present, to acknowledge the successful completion of the project. We celebrated with speeches, book signings, and toasts with glasses of wine.

Your Next Steps In Being a Collaborative Leader

There is a structure to collaborating. There are specific steps and stages that govern how people come together to solve a problem and/or create a compelling new future. So, in any and every collaborative adventure, you should know the steps that make up your journey and where you are in the process.

If you are already collaborating with others on a project, where are you now? Which of the collaborative steps are you most skilled and competent in, and which are you least skilled in? What talents and skills do you need to find in others who could contribute to the collaborative partnership?

Chapter 6

Calling For and Inspiring Collaboration

Inviting Others

We are caught up in an inescapable network of mutuality, tied to a single garment of destiny. Whatever affects one directly, affects all indirectly.

Martin Luther King

None of us is as smart as all of us.

Anon.

Collaboration is a passion, not a mere cohabitation. Where there is no real passion, there will be no real collaboration.

When it comes to the actual process of collaborating, certain skills are required if we want to create a healthy and robust collaboration. High quality collaborations do not just happen; they are designed and created. Certain core competencies make collaboration possible. What are these core competencies? Right now, we want to focus on five of those competencies:

1. The *call* for collaboration whereby we invite others to collaborate.
2. The *courage* to put ourselves out there in making the offer to collaborate.
3. The *choice* about whether to collaborate.
4. The *culture* that we create which supports the collaborative partnership or community.
5. The *connecting and combining* of the differences that we and others bring to the collaboration to generate a synergy.

These will be the themes of this chapter and the following three chapters, which will detail the essential skills needed to create a collaboration. Let's begin here with the call to collaboration because that's where it all begins.

Living An Itinerant Collaborative Life

If there was ever anyone who lived his life by collaborating it was Paul Erdős. Dr. Erdős was a prodigiously gifted and productive mathematician who Charles Krauthammer describes in these words:

> Erdos' whole life was so improbable no novelist could have invented him. As chronicled by Paul Hoffman in *The Atlantic Monthly*, Erdos had no home, no family, no possessions, no address. He went from math conference to math conference, from university to university, knocking on the doors of mathematicians throughout the world, declaring, "My brain is open" and moved in. His colleagues, grateful for a few days' collaboration with Erdos—his mathematical breadth was as impressive as his depth—took him in. (2013, p. 25)

Paul Erdős traveled with only two suitcases, carrying in them everything he owned—some clothes and mathematical papers. Yet, by the end of his life, from collaborating with hundreds of scientists and mathematicians, he had produced more than 1,500 mathematical papers: "An astonishing legacy in a field where a lifetime product of 50 papers is considered quite extraordinary" (Krauthammer, 1996).

Erdős was unlike so many geniuses who are eccentric to the point of becoming antisocial and totally absorbed in a private world—for example, Bobby Fischer and Howard Hughes. Krauthammer describes Erdős as being:

> gentle, open, and generous with others. He believed in making mathematics a social activity. Indeed, he was the most prolifically collaborative mathematician in history. Hundreds of colleagues who have published with him or been advised by him can trace some breakthrough or insight to an evening with Erdos, brain open. That sociability sets him apart from other mathematical geniuses. (2013, p. 26)

The key to the collaborative leadership that Erdős demonstrated was his openness—he said "my brain is open." This helped to make him a lifelong learner and distinguished him from many mathematicians who bloom early and then fade. At 83 he was still learning and making original contributions. By his social openness he made himself available for collaborations. He made the call to collaboration by simply showing up at someone's door, ringing the doorbell, and saying, "I'm here to collaborate, I've got an idea … When do we get started?"

The Core Competency of Inviting

Collaborations typically begin with an inspiration. An individual or a group gets an idea and from that stimulus they call upon others to join them in a collaborative effort to turn the inspirational vision into a reality. Most collaborations begin in this way.

The collaboration can be led by an individual or a group (a leadership team). The leaders invite or call people (and groups) to be part of the collaboration. They start the collaboration by inviting it. Seeing the possibility, they then make the request. Without someone to see the possibility and make the request, the collaboration will not happen.

Inviting others to join a collaboration is what it takes to begin. What could be more simple or obvious? But don't let simple and obvious deceive you. To invite a collaboration requires many of the essential ingredients that make up the best in leadership: vision, courage, risk-taking, trust, belief in people, and stepping out.

There are two kinds of collaborative relationship which you might ask others to join or be invited to join yourself. First, there is the instrumental collaborative relationship. This is a time limited and ad hoc coming together of individuals to collaborate for a purpose—a purpose that will come to an end at some point. Because this kind of collaboration requires an exit strategy, it is always best to expect and plan for its termination from the beginning. Second, there is the visionary collaborative relationship. This involves a legacy that goes beyond yourself and perhaps even your time. This collaboration does not end but continues to evolve and change as it moves into the future. It requires the grooming of leaders so that others can carry on the collective product or service.

After I (LMH) had completed the *Innovations In NLP* book with Shelle Rose Charvet, we were asked many questions about our collaboration and the collaboration we had created with leaders in the field of NLP. People wanted to know: How did it begin? Who first got the idea for you guys to get together on that project? How did all of you come together originally? What was the original impetus that sparked the idea of collaborating?

We had observed that usually there is one key person who steps into the role of "inviter." That person sees the need or the vision and makes the original invitation for others to work together. From time to time, two or three people might jointly recognize the same need and act as if in unison. This happened with Shelle Rose Charvet and I on our first collaboration, which resulted in *Innovations In NLP*. I initiated the project because I felt the need to collaborate in the field of NLP and because I had written a critique of a particular book which I felt failed to create a "world where everyone felt welcomed."

Upon reading my review, Shelle contacted me, and even though she also felt the same need, she believed my approach was more reactive than proactive. She said that it amounted to "criticism without a solution." As I listened to her, I had to agree. She was right. Then she challenged me: "Why don't you do something about it?" I thought that was a great idea, even though I didn't know exactly what I could do. But I was willing to explore what could be done and then take action if that was possible. Having been challenged, I turned it round on Shelle, "I will do something about it if you will help me and if you will be a part of making it happen." Later, at the book launch in London, she said that her inner response to my counter-question, was "Oh, shit!" And that's how that collaboration began!

The Power of An Invitation

Until the three of us (Michael, Ian, and Shelle) studied and modeled collaboration, none of us fully appreciated the power contained within an invitation. But within every successful collaboration there is an invitation. Someone, at some time, invites one or more people to join together to address a need. The power within this is subtle, sometimes very subtle, as when someone remarks in an offhand manner, "What do you think about the idea to …?" The power in the invitation is that it releases people to start thinking about collaborating together on something which they had never before considered. Without the invitation, the generalized impulse to do something often fades away and comes to nothing.

The invitation to collaborate is an act of faith because it arises from the conviction that we can do something about a need or a vision, that we can achieve more and better together than we can alone, and that we can trust and depend on others to achieve a vision. At the same time, the invitation is an act of courage. Someone has to make the invitation and, while we don't have statistics on this, our experience suggests that many, maybe most, invitations are not acted on, not believed, not trusted, or downright criticized or rejected. Such invitations are often pooh-poohed as being too unrealistic, too time consuming, and not having sufficient resources.

Perhaps this is why, many times, the invitation doesn't come knocking on the door and announcing, "I'm inviting you to collaborate in a great project that will change the world!" Rather, it comes as hints, vague suggestions, and offhand comments in the spur of a moment. It may even come as a joke while you're sharing a glass of wine. "Wouldn't it be something if we combined forces and did something really big?" "Here's a crazy idea, what if we got Joe and Brenda to help us out with this?" "The other day I got to wondering what a company that combined Microsoft and Apple would look like ..."

The bottom line is that someone has to initiate the invitation to collaborate. In his best-selling book, *The Tipping Point* (2000), Malcolm Gladwell identified the maven, the connector, and the salesperson as the three key critical roles for a grassroots social change movement. Of these roles, it is the connector who first connects people together by making the invitation to collaborate.

The Courage To Make the Call

What does it take, if you have an idea, to call others to join a collaboration? Certainly it requires passion and excitement but it also requires a good deal of courage. After all, you might be laughed at, mocked, turned down, rejected, or worse. If you've got an idea, goal, or vision that is too big for one person to achieve, then the next step is to figure out who already naturally shares that idea or vision. Sometimes this means "throwing out many seeds upon the waters" to see where they go and who responds.[1] You do this when you really

---

1   This phrase comes from Ecclesiastes 11:1: "Cast your bread upon the waters, for you will find it after many days."

do not know who else may be thinking along the same lines or who else may share your passion.

I (LMH) find that calling for a collaboration is an easy and natural way of being in the world. After I began researching this book with Ian, I realized that for years I had been throwing out ideas and possibilities for numerous collaborations with a wide range of people. When I had a private psychotherapy practice in the small town where I live in Colorado, I did this to be a part of something bigger than myself and to stay challenged and on the cutting edge of psychotherapy. I not only joined associations of psychotherapists and played an active part in those groups, but I also invited others to join me in some experimental exercises that I had read about (e.g., "Let's set up a hidden mirror in a therapy room and watch each other to give feedback for improvement") and I would also invite myself onto their projects. Sometimes this suggestion was warmly accepted; at other times they seemed to look at me as if I was a visitor from another planet!

Sometimes, however, calling for a collaboration demands being more strategic. It means studying to find out who else is discussing the need or vision, interviewing people who might know about it, researching what is already known, and finding out who is already working in the area. Often, you may find that a leader or a group has already been established, so now the invitation may be your invitation to join them.

Choosing the Call You'll Make For a Collaboration

If calling for collaboration is a core competency, and courageously acting to make the call is another, then the third skill is choosing to collaborate. After all, there are lots of choices and lots of decisions to make:

- What do I want to collaborate on or about?
- What do I care about and feel a passion for taking on with others?
- Do I launch out and make the call, or do I find others who have already started and courageously join them?
- When I (or we) have an idea, when do we start the collaboration and how do we go about the launch?
- Is this a short-term ad hoc collaboration or a long-term one?
- When do we anticipate the collaboration will end?

- Am I ready to collaborate? Am I personally prepared, mentally and emotionally, to enter into a collaboration?
- Do I (or we) have an exit plan, or end game, in mind so that we can end the collaboration as gracefully as we began it?
- Do I (or we) have the communication skills to clarify our goals and methods in the collaboration, or do we need to collaborate about that first?

Within the call, then, there are lots of choices you will make—about what, where, when, who, and possibly how. There will be choices about values, criteria, standards, style, and chemistry.

Leading the Call

There are several leadership roles that a collaborative leader will need to take on at the beginning of a collaboration. These are the roles of inviter, visionary, and planner. He or she does this by presenting a vision that identifies opportunities and then invites, requests, and galvanizes people to get behind it. The vision should inspire, invigorate, and align people, as well as providing an awareness of what, why, and how to do it.

As a collaborative leader, a necessary skill is that of recognizing excellence in others. Bennis describes what it means to be a strong leader when leading a collaboration:

> The ability to recognize excellence in others and their work may be the defining talent of leaders of great groups. ... Such leaders are like great conductors. They may not be able to play Mozart's First Violin Concerto, but they have a profound understanding of the work and can create the environment needed to realize it. (1997, p. 200)

Recognizing excellence in others obviously requires the ability to look for it. It's amazing how much we miss because we're not even looking. So, a willingness to look (even hunt) for talent and skills and imagine gifts in others is essential. Even more rare is the ability to see it when it is in embryonic form—before it is developed. For that you have to develop a belief about other people's potential.

Quality Collaboration

When inviting and forecasting the collaboration pathway, there are four key variables that we have identified in effective collaborations:

1. *Care*: A passion for something bigger than yourself as a single individual.
2. *Trust*: A respect for the skills, knowledge, and competencies of others.
3. *Work*: A vision of a task that is tremendously important and that requires the effort of many people.
4. *Joy*: The fun of doing something that is highly significant.

The diagrams below illustrate how the interface between these diverse mental and emotional states—care (passion), trust (respect), work (task/effort), and joy (fun)—come together to create a new emergent quality. This is indicated by the asterisk (*)—the singularity that arises. It is this singularity experience that creates something more than, and different from, all of the contributing factors.

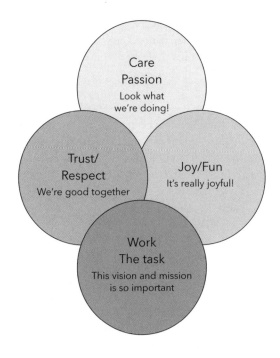

The Dimensions of Collaboration

In the first area we have Care + Trust + Work, but no joy. Here is joyless collaboration.

In the second area we have Joy + Care + Work, but no trust or respect. Here we have distrustful collaboration.

In the third area we have Work + Trust + Joy, but no passion or genuine care. This gives us passionless collaboration.

In the fourth area of overlap (*) we have Care + Joy + Work + Trust. This gives us optimal collaboration.

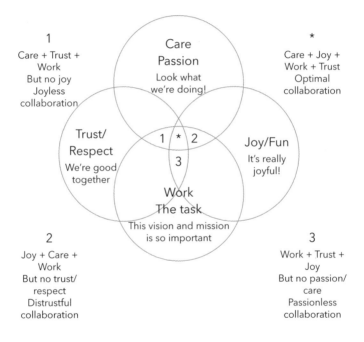

1
Care + Trust +
Work
But no joy
Joyless
collaboration

*
Care + Joy +
Work + Trust
Optimal
collaboration

Care
Passion
Look what
we're doing!

Trust/
Respect
We're good
together

Joy/Fun
It's really
joyful!

Work
The task
This vision and mission
is so important

2
Joy + Care +
Work
But no trust/
respect
Distrustful
collaboration

3
Work + Trust +
Joy
But no passion/
care
Passionless
collaboration

Your Next Steps In Being a Collaborative Leader

There is always someone (or a group of people) who will start a collaboration around a goal or project. Will it be you? Will you step up?

You now know about the first three core competencies for collaboration: calling others to join you in a collaborative project, courageously stepping up to invite others or ask to join them, and choosing the details of when, how, who, and why of your collaboration. How good are you at these three skills?

If someone doesn't speak up and ask others to join together for a collaborative vision, it will not happen. The possibility will be missed. How many collaborations that could have occurred—which people thought about, dreamed about, and talked about—never happened? Why not? Because no one started it. Now you know that collaborations come into being through invitations, what subtle invitations do you realize you have received from someone? What invitations have you made or do you now need to make?

Chapter 7

Choosing To Collaborate

Making the Decision

We must do the things we think we cannot do.
Eleanor Roosevelt, *You Learn By Living* (1960)

These leaders see themselves less as soloists than as collaborators. Leaders and followers are engaged in the same dance.
Warren Bennis, *On Becoming a Leader* (2003)

Will you or won't you collaborate? If you and/or others have an idea or project in mind, and you have talked through the possibilities, then ultimately the time will come to make a choice: Will you or won't you make the decision to collaborate? If you decide to make this choice, it is at this point that the collaboration begins. After all, collaborations don't just happen—they are chosen. People who have a vision, and talk about it, come to a point where they say, "Okay, let's do it!" They make a commitment to begin.

Every collaboration also has an endpoint. Just as there was the day when you got together and put your heads and hearts together to collaborate on an exciting project, so too, for most collaborations, the day arrives when the project comes to an end. Then, too, we make a decision that it is time to recognize, honor, and celebrate the culmination of this particular collaboration.

We ended Chapter 6 by identifying the key choices that are wrapped up within a collaboration, although there are also many smaller decisions involved in making the initial request to collaborate. We now move to the initiating decision. This is the big decision about actually choosing to collaborate and the resolve to make a go of it.

What Do You Bring To the Collaboration?

Imagine a battery made out of wood. Preposterous, right? Well, Assistant Professor Lianbing Hu and his colleagues have been working on just that.[1] The battery, which is being developed at the Energy Research Center at the University of Maryland, is currently in prototype form, but Dr. Hu's team are continuing to fine-tune the design until they have something commercially viable.

This story appeared on the nation-wide radio program, PRN, in July 2013. What caught my (LMH) attention was something about those who came up with this idea. That's because one of the authors on the research paper describing the project in *Nano Letters* was an undergraduate. As I listened to the report, I wondered how it was that a young undergraduate student managed to get his name on a major scientific paper as a co-author? That's pretty amazing.

At first, engineering major Nicholas Weadock assisted in the lab by helping Dr. Hu's PhD students with their English grammar, many of whom were from outside the US. But Hu discovered that young Weadock was asking some very insightful questions about the science behind the work. His original focus had been wind power but he later became interested in energy storage technology and wanted to show Dr. Hu that he could make a valuable contribution to his research.

In this surprising collaboration, what did Weadock bring to the collaboration? He brought intense curiosity focused questions, a commitment to learning, and a willingness to collaborate.

Decision-Making Strategies

How do you decide? You decide based on the pros and cons to enter into a collaboration. Your decision will also be based on the advantages and disadvantages of staying as you are. How does it weigh out for you? Which way do the scales tip in terms of the values, standards, and criteria that you use to weigh the pros and cons on each side of the decision?

In any decision-making process there are the specific pros and cons for both making and not making a particular choice. Above those details are the values that you use as your criteria. These are your standards by which you determine the significance of the potential collaboration.

---

1   Joe Palca writes about Dr. Hu's project in his article, "All Charged Up: Engineers Create a Battery Made of Wood" (2013). He explains that the "wood" is actually "microscopic wood fibers that are fashioned into thin sheets." The sheets are coated with carbon nanotubes and packed into small metal discs. The wood batteries use sodium ions rather than lithium ions which are found in normal batteries.

Every decision involves pros and cons. If there weren't lots of advantages to collaborating, or at least a strong dominating one, we wouldn't choose to do it. But there are also disadvantages because with every decision that we say yes to we are required to say no to other things.

When making a decision, it is typical for people to think about the benefits or advantages and compare them to the costs or disadvantages. When we do this, we say things such as, "On the one hand, it would save time or money. It would prevent redundancy and the reinvention of the wheel. But, on the other hand, there will be a steep learning curve and that will take a lot of initial time as we begin."

A more strategic approach is to write down the pros and cons in two columns.[2]

	Advantages +	Disadvantages −
If I go with the decision:		
Weight of emotional value		
If I don't make the decision:		
Weight of emotional value		

The amazing thing with this technique is that it frees your mind to think about other items. It also gives you the opportunity to plant several questions in your mind:

- What else? What are other benefits?
- What are other disadvantages?
- What standards do I want to use to govern my decisions?
- What is important to me in deciding on any given collaboration?

When you have a full list, you can gauge the importance of each item on a scale from 0 to 10. Rating each item allows you to add up the numbers in each column to see how the advantages and

---

2   For more about decision-making, see Chapter 12 of Hall (2015a) on provoking change. The following table comes from this chapter and from the training manual on Module III of Meta-Coaching.

disadvantages weigh out against each other. If the sides are pretty even, the weight of each will balance out like a scale (typically, this explains the indecision).

Next, explore the criteria you have consciously or unconsciously used in making your evaluations:

- What standards, values, or rules have you used to come up with your ratings?
- What is important to you? What do you value?
- Are these standards ecological for you?
- What do you dis-value?
- As you step back from your criteria, what is your objective?
- What are your goals and outcomes?
- Do your goals and outcomes serve you well? Do they bring out the best in you?

Once you've worked through your decision-making strategy in terms of the content items that you've listed, scaled, and weighed, you can now explore your style of decision-making.[3]

- How many times do you need to consider a decision before you are ready to make the choice? Do you make the choice the first time, after three times, seven times, or never?
- Does the decision need to be coded in a certain format? Do you need to see the items written out, say them to yourself, or count them off on your fingers (i.e., visual, auditory, kinesthetic)?
- Do you have an identity that supports you in making a clear-cut decision? Does your self-image enable you to think of yourself as a decisive person? Or are you an indecisive person? Do you need to shift your self-image so that you can be more decisive?
- When you make a decision, do you stay with it? Is it solid and robust, or does it fade away and you go back to re-deciding all over again?

---

3   These considerations involve what are called "meta-programs" in NLP. For more about meta-programs, see Hall and Bodenhamer (2005). For more about decision-making, see the decision conversation in Hall (2015a).

Leading the Decision

When you lead people to a decision, you present the vision and then make the proposal in such a way that the value of the collaboration sells itself. People will want to sign up and be part of the team. One challenge in this process will be not to go too fast. Making the decision cannot be just a matter of emotional excitement. Merely feeling excited and passionate about something is, by itself, an inadequate method for making a smart choice.

In order to get robust commitment to the collaboration, as a collaborative leader you will need to enable people to weigh the pros and cons and consider the true cost of the project. By ensuring that people make a solid and smart decision—one which fits their values and life situation—you then enroll only individuals who will come through on their decision to be an active part of the collaboration.

Be warned: This can be a lengthy and time consuming process. And because people need to talk out significant decisions and feel heard, it requires a lot of patience and grace on the part of the leader. However, this process lies at the very core of how to win minds and hearts. Furthermore, as individuals, we all take different amounts of time to try on an idea and live with it for long enough to feel comfortable with it.

It also takes time because leading the decision requires that we collect pertinent information from as many parties as will be affected by the collaboration. We will never obtain all of the necessary facts and data, but we need to gather as much relevant and accurate information as possible.

Choosing to participate in a collaboration does not end with the initial decision that launches the adventure. After that there will be many decisions along the way which will energize the original decision and give it legs. This is because when you choose to collaborate, you are choosing to be responsible *for* yourself, to be accountable *to* others, and to share authority. You are opting to share knowledge and information and be transparent with your collaborators.

Choosing To End a Collaboration

Every collaboration has an endpoint. Just as there came the day to get together, put your heads and hearts together to collaborate on an exciting project, so too the day will come when the project comes to a close. What then? How do we graciously and effectively end a collaboration that has made such a positive difference in our lives?

We collaborate for a purpose: to achieve something together that we cannot achieve alone or apart. So, naturally, when we have accomplished our collective outcome, the collaboration will come to an end. By beginning with the end in mind, you will build into the plan an exit strategy that will define when and how you will bring closure to the collaboration. Make sure to recognize and honor the successes that you have achieved together. How will you do this? Will you plan a celebration event at the end to recognize all of the people who have played key roles? Will you throw a party?

Your Next Steps In Being a Collaborative Leader

When you have an opportunity to be collaborative, how will you decide that the decision to participate in the project or to lead the collaboration is the right one for you? What will you use as your criteria regarding that particular shared vision so that you can know if it does or does not fit for you? Being clear now will enable you to be more ready when you recognize an opportunity when it arises.

- Will it correspond to your life vision and mission?
- What is your vision and mission?
- Will it correspond to your lifestyle?
- How do you describe the way you live your life?
- Do you have the time, energy, and skills for it?

Chapter 8

Creating a Culture of Collaboration

Collaboration Inside Out

The most important thing anyone could do to foster collaboration was to begin acting in a trustworthy and a trusting way. ... The most successful leaders are invariably collaborators. They know they can't do it all on their own. That means they need to work effectively with others.

Ian McDermott, *Boost Your Confidence with NLP* (2010)

Collaborative efforts ... demand a new form of leadership that transform the notion of leadership itself.

David Chrislip

Within an organization, it takes a very special culture to support collaboration. In many businesses, collaboration cannot only *not* work, it cannot even get started. Many companies have a culture that suffers from being anti-collaborative; the invitation to collaborate, if it is even heard, is immediately rejected or discounted. Why? Because there is something in the way in the current culture. It could be that a range of things are counteracting collaboration, such as competition, scarcity, suspicion, partisan politics, or hierarchical structures. There is the view, "That's not the way we do things around here so, no, I don't want to do that!"

So, if there are cultures (in businesses, families, ethnic/religious groups, etc.) where collaboration isn't countenanced, what kind of environment *is* required for collaboration to work? What kind of culture *does* encourage collaboration to grow and thrive? If you are a collaborative leader, do you know how to facilitate an atmosphere that openly welcomes collaboration?

The Culture For Collaboration

In order to support collaboration, you will need to nurture a very special environment that will both inspire and empower people. This culture should emphasize the importance of seven key elements: abundance, win-win thinking, entrepreneurship, trust, vision, receptiveness, and responsibility.

1. Abundance

Collaboration thrives when there is a win-win attitude. One of the key beliefs supporting this kind of thinking is the idea that everyone can benefit (we call this an "abundance mindset") and then operating from this mindset. This shifts the old zero-sum game to one of synergy and success. It means believing that my win does not have to mean a loss for anyone else—it can actually mean a win for them too. In contrast, scarcity thinking assumes that the pie is only so big and everybody who takes something from it diminishes what is available for everybody else. While this kind of thinking is valid in certain tangible cases (but, even then, not always), it is completely fallacious when applied to intangible resources.

The use of an intangible resource can create even more of that resource. For example, the more you learn and know, the more you can learn and know. The resource of learning and understanding is not diminished when you pass on your learning and knowledge to someone else. You are not impoverished such that you have less knowledge—you actually have more. Furthermore, the very process of using your knowledge means you will be learning more and increasing the quality and quantity of your understanding. This means that, in giving away what you know, you actually expand your capacity for knowledge. The same applies to love and compassion, to leading and managing, to respect and curiosity.

When we think from the frame of abundance, we see that using an intangible resource, or giving an intangible experience, creates more—and it creates a new and powerful perception. It generates a fundamental optimism in the nature of the world, a belief in a brighter future, and a commitment to building that more hopeful future. The premise is that we live (or could live) in a world of abundance—an abundance of ideas, creativity, possibilities, respect, love, learning, growth, and so on. The more we create these experiences, the more experiences we can create. Abundance is a "the more–the more" pattern.

The premise of abundance originates in Abraham Maslow's work into the psychology of human nature and shows up in what he termed the "B-needs" (being). Conversely, the idea of scarcity—which leads to competition, an ego-centered focus, one-upmanship, the urge to win, the need to be right, the inability to acknowledge the contributions of others, the failure to groom leaders, kingdom-building around egos, and many other destructive forces—arises from living in the realm of the D-needs (deficiency).

2. Win-Win Thinking

From abundance thinking emerges the collaborative idea that everybody can win. This kind of thinking is committed to everyone winning and is willing to do whatever it takes so that everyone can win. Equally, if we don't believe that everyone can win, if we are not committed to it, if we do not organize things so that it will happen, then it won't.

The opposite of win-win thinking is win-lose thinking. This kind of reasoning puts people at odds with each other and elicits competitive rather than collaborative behavior. Win-win thinking means that our purpose in collaborating is not trying to be number one or to win *over* others. It is about wanting to win *with* others and to be a part of a winning team.

This is what the quality control expert, W. Edwards Deming, did with his revolutionary approach to quality. Instead of running a quality control *after* the creation of a product, he shifted the focus in the manufacturing process to how employees can work together to produce quality products *during* the process. What today seems common sense was groundbreaking thinking when he suggested that workers become a team and manage the quality themselves. This essential collaboration framework revolutionized businesses in Japan, and then in the United States, and after that the rest of the world. The idea that workers could be responsible for collaboratively designing and integrating quality into the process was at first extreme, even radical, and then later it was just good business sense.

3. Entrepreneurship

Collaboration arises, grows, and succeeds in cultures that are entrepreneurial in nature. It's an environment where being an entrepreneur, thinking like an entrepreneur, and behaving like an entrepreneur is encouraged, validated, and rewarded. This means taking personal responsibility and thinking about the success of the entire enterprise. Without this attitude people will not collaborate; they will compete.

Collaboration, like entrepreneurship, involves experimenting, taking risks, trying new things, stepping out into new areas without any guarantees, and thinking out of the box in unconventional ways. When a group operates in this way, there is a need for mutual support. The opposite of this is bureaucratic thinking, which is safety and security oriented and focuses on control rather than mutual support for smart risk-taking.

At the center of entrepreneurial thinking is an assumption of personal responsibility. The reason the entrepreneur is proactive, responsive, takes the initiative, and values responsibility is that she recognizes and owns her personal ability to respond to events. When collaborators come together with this kind of thinking, and they add this to their interactions, they create a mutual sense of accountable responsibility. This empowers their collaboration and makes it workable.

Entrepreneurship presupposes the variables that are inherent in creativity. This includes the ability to embrace the ambiguous and confusing, the willingness to try new things (to test things and experiment), and an openness of mind to look at things in unconventional ways. In a collaboration, all of this makes the experience highly stimulating intellectually. Then the group itself becomes creative and able to innovate new ideas fairly easily.

4. Trust

For win-win thinking and entrepreneurship to arise and thrive in an organization, there has to be trust—loads of trust. Start by assuming that people are trustworthy and trusting and use this as your modus operandi. Only then will trust be made operational in how colleagues relate to each other, and only then will a high quality of collaboration emerge. Without a foundation of trust, collaboration will be stifled because individuals will hold back. They will look upon proposals to collaborate with suspicion and apprehension. Even worse, they will treat that invitation with distrust. When people are wary of each other, and the processes of communicating and working together, collaboration doesn't have a chance to blossom.

In *The Speed of Trust*, Stephen Covey describes trust as the "bedrock" of collaboration:

Forbes highlighted this "collaboration as opportunity" trend in 2006, pointing out what they call the "bedrock" of collaboration: trust. Without trust, collaboration is merely cooperation, which fails to achieve the benefits and possibilities available to true collaborators in the knowledge worker age. (2006, p. 256)

In my book, *Boost Your Confidence with NLP*, I (Ian) wrote the following about trust and leadership:

The most successful leaders are invariably collaborators. They know they can't do it all on their own. That means they need to work effectively with others. Some of the biggest decisions you will need to make at work—and make with confidence—will revolve around collaboration.

Ultimately collaboration comes down to trust. Can you trust those you're working with? That raises a whole bunch of questions at lots of different Logical Levels. Can you trust their honesty and integrity (Identity); their judgment (Belief); their skill level (Capability); and can you trust them to deliver in particular circumstances (Behavior and Environment)?

Over twenty years ago, I founded an organization called International Teaching Seminars. It has gone from strength to strength and is now recognized as the most successful NLP and coaching organization in the world. I had the vision and I am the founder, but the reason it is still going strong today is that there is a team running it. The people I work with, I work *with*. They have an amazing collaborative spirit, they'll cover for each other, argue vigorously with each other—and me! … If I look at my own evolution over these years, I would say that one of the great lessons for me has been not only to delegate more but also to trust more.

Confident collaboration leads to *smarter* working. Nobody works in a bubble; knowing how to work with other people is a skill you will be able to apply in every job and every workplace you land in. (2010, pp. 132–133)

5. Inspirational Vision

A prerequisite for all of these elements to be operational in a given culture is the presence of an inspirational vision. Without a governing vision that excites, thrills, delights, and captivates people's hearts and minds, collaboration will not make sense. Where there is such a vision, we collaborate in service of the vision. The vision pulls us together and unifies us. We collaborate in order to be able to achieve something much bigger and bolder than what we could accomplish alone.

People want to collaborate and play with each other when there is a bigger game to play, when we are part of something larger than ourselves. One of the central roles for a collaborative leader, if not the most central role, is to inspire people to the vision of a bigger game.

6. Receptiveness To Others and To New Ideas

Openness to each other is required for trust, for win-win thinking, for taking risks, and much more. People who are closed and rigid do not make good collaborators. This is because they hold back, they keep information close to their chest, and they keep secrets. All of these things inevitably undermine collaboration.

To effectively collaborate you have to open yourself up to new ideas and to other people. This means being open and receptive to one another. This highlights another fear inherent in collaboration: openness means making yourself vulnerable to being wronged, being hurt, and being taken advantage of. However, when open receptivity dominates a culture's communication, then the communication itself becomes richer, fuller, and more plenteous.

Receptiveness implies that people are also open to having fun and being playful. Again, these are variables of creativity, entrepreneurship, and trust. When things are enjoyable, playful, and exciting, people are more flexible and more able to adjust to changing circumstances.

Receptiveness also denotes authenticity. We are only truly open to each other and receptive of working together when we are willing to put aside all of the roles, masks, and personas that we live behind—that is, when we find the courage to come out from behind ourselves and be real. This isn't easy and it doesn't happen quickly. However, when we have more experiences of being trusted and trustworthy, we begin to trust each other and become more authentic in our interactions.

7. Being Responsive and Responsible

Finally, a collaborative culture must have a strong sense of empowerment. Only then will people feel able to be responsive and step up to being responsible. When they feel empowered and strong enough in themselves to be held accountable for what they say and do, they will want to be held accountable. Without this factor in the culture, the collaboration will have no backbone and no strength. When people fail to do what they have promised, and are not held accountable, the collaboration weakens and becomes unsustainable.

To create a culture that is characterized by responsibility, we need high quality, sensory based feedback to all and from all. This is about the ability to confront each other about anything and everything that undermines the collaboration. When we have this, we have a process whereby we can keep the collaboration authentic and up to date.

When people feel personally responsible, they refrain from blaming others when something goes wrong. They do not blame other people or external factors; instead, they assume responsibility for their own actions and responses. Where there is blaming, and therefore a lack of ownership, a negative environment emerges which encourages people to clam up and not to reveal problems or potential problems. As a result, mistakes and flaws are feared and dreaded, and people worry about being blamed.

Responsibility also entails and leads to proactivity. This means being tenacious. It entails persistence in staying with something and dealing with difficulties. It means persevering until we achieve our goals. The "never give up" attitude of tenacity shows up in refusing to let adversity stop you or kill your dream.

How To Create a Collaborative Culture

As we have seen, for a highly effective collaboration we first need a culture of collaboration. But how do we create a culture of collaboration? It is all about discipline. Here are some of the fundamental elements required to create an effective culture of collaboration.

Establish Dialogue With Everyone In the Organization Or Group

Make it clear that dialogue is the way your organization (or group) learns together and communicates. Discuss your collaboration with colleagues, as this will enable you to establish an ongoing collaborative conversation. Then together you can collaborate conversationally about how you will achieve your shared goal. If you use Socratic inquiry and questions, you will be able to learn together as a group and co-create a shared vision that will galvanize you all. Dialogue will enable you to build mutual understanding which, of course, is the foundation for collaboration. If you want individuals to feel part of something, you have to give them a voice; otherwise, they will feel it has been imposed upon them without their input.

Build An Inside-Out Culture

When you begin to develop the kind of culture that will support authentic collaboration, make sure that you start on the inside. Do this by taking the initiative as a collaborative leader and inviting others into the collaboration. You will probably want to present and/or co-create some initial ground rules which will set you up to establish a successful collaboration.

As you create your inside-out culture, ensure that all the key stakeholders are present. Who are the stakeholders and are they all involved? How will you reach potential stakeholders so that their voices are included? How will you make decisions as a group? How will you make decisions when you do not have unanimity or consensus? All of this is important, or you will set things up so that one or a few stakeholders can hold the collaborative group hostage because only their voices are being heard and only their demands are being considered.

Integrate Collaborative Principles

We have already looked at some of the essential principles of collaboration, such as operating from abundance, sharing, playing well with others, minding your manners, and so on. (For more on this see the self-assessment questionnaire in Appendix A.) Use these principles to create a civil context in which to handle differences and hot topics. Synergy is especially important when creating a community based on win-win interactions. All of these principles need to be integrated into the thinking, emoting, speaking, behaving, and relating of people so that you create a cooperative culture that supports a common way of working together.

Regularly and Consistently Talk About the Vision

It is critical to get into the habit of conversing about your vision on an ongoing basis. This frames the vision as central and keeps it in everyone's mind as the group's operating principle. As obvious as this seems, it is amazingly easy to get so involved in all the day-to-day demands that your attention dominates and crowds out your inspirational intentions.

Your Next Steps In Being a Collaborative Leader

For collaboration to emerge and flourish, we have to start with the right context and environment—that is, the right culture. Culture simply refers to how we cultivate our mind, emotion, speech, and behavior to create the mental and emotional contexts of our lives. If we don't like how our minds and emotions have been cultivated, it is up to us to develop a new style. We can create a new collaborative culture.

If you are ready to cultivate a new cultural environment, then you will want to make sure that you facilitate the seven qualities we have detailed in this chapter. Here is a checklist you might want to use to score yourself on a 0–10 scale to determine what you want to do next to become more effective as a collaborative leader.

- I believe in abundance and in the synergy of abundance.
- I engage in win-win thinking on a regular basis when interacting with others.

- I think of myself as an entrepreneur and engage in entrepreneurial activities.
- I am trustworthy and know how to trust.
- I have an inspirational vision and communicate it regularly to others.
- I operate from an open receptiveness to others and to new ideas.
- I am responsive to others and assume responsibility for the conditions of my life.

Chapter 9

Combining Differences For Synergy

Welcoming and Integrating

You can't improve collaboration until you've addressed the issue of conflict.

L. Michael Hall

Ultimately collaboration comes down to trust. Can you trust those you're working with?

Ian McDermott

A consistent theme throughout this book is that collaboration arises from differences and thrives through differences. Collaboration embraces differences in order to fully utilize them. No wonder, then, that we want and need diversity. The only kind of collaboration that is actually worthy of the name is a collaboration made up of different people with different perspectives, different skills, different styles and ways of going about things, and different ideas and suggestions, all working together for a common goal and mutual vision.

Without differences, everybody will be thinking, talking, and acting as if they are clones of one another. But the purpose of collaboration is not to create clones. What could be more boring? What could be less productive? If everybody is the same, then only one person is needed and all others are redundant.

> Wisdom comes from sitting together and truthfully confronting our differences, without the intention to change anything.
> **Gregory Bateson, *Steps To An Ecology of Mind* (1972)**

Collaboration, by its very nature, is a synergy of differences. Difference is what fuels collaboration to be dynamic and is the source of new creative ideas. So collaboration, by definition, involves pulling together people with various values, skills, and understandings. This is why collaboration is not the same as consensus and why consensus is actually an enemy of collaboration. After all, consensus is a process that seeks to eliminate differences by getting everyone to agree. Typically, this results in everyone compromising on important distinctions and values.

But collaborating with a wide range of individuals is not easy. If it was collaboration would happen more often, it would be successful more often, and it would not be feared or avoided as it often is. If synergizing differences was simple, there would be less conflict, less fighting over control, less bureaucracy, and less of the ruthless kind of competition we see so often.

Effective collaboration confronts, challenges, and changes basic perceptions about others, and it does so by recognizing the power of conversation to create community. Conversations provide the means to build societies of respect, tolerance, justice, responsibility, and compassion. In this way, we generate true communities where there is a sense of belonging, a respect for difference (e.g., respect, care, love), and the ability to tap into and unleash human potentials to achieve our highest aspirations.

As a collaborative leader, the challenge is, how do you embrace difference when you lead a collaboration? How skilled are you, as a collaborative leader, in welcoming, utilizing, and synergizing differences? The skills essential for leading a synergistic collaboration include accepting and respecting differences, adopting the language of collaboration, structuring to integrate differences, and effectively dealing with conflict.

Accepting Differences—The Heart of Collaboration

The core competency of collaborative leadership is acceptance. This means welcoming and respecting differences so they can be integrated into the group. This requires the ability to look beyond surface dissimilarities and to accept and appreciate the fact that no individual is perfect, no mental map is perfect, and no style is perfect. But something more is required: leaders also need to recognize that a collaborative partnership requires multiple mental maps and numerous styles. The differing mental maps of people in a collaboration give us a richer perspective and enable us to hold together what would otherwise be contradictory.

> The real role of the leader is to figure out how you make diverse people and elements work together.
> **Warren Bennis,** *On Becoming a Leader* **(2003)**

Welcoming differences begins with an acknowledgment that, in most situations, there can be several versions of the "truth." This enables us to look at a situation from multiple perspectives, and is what Gregory Bateson described as the structure and essence of wisdom. Looking at a singular issue or event from different points of view adds richness to the texture of the whole.

How easy or hard do you find it to accept and embrace differences? To find out, use the permission process described below.

The Permission Process

If there is anything prohibiting, forbidding, or "tabooing" your behavior, such that you experience a psychological "can't" (e.g., "I can't trust others," "I can't stand differences," "I can't stand criticism or conflict"), then the following process may help you to free yourself from this mental frame. These types of frames cause us to live in a restricted mental-emotional space which doesn't allow us to move out into the prohibited or taboo area.

1. Check Your Inner Permission
Find a quiet place, go within, and say the following words of permission to yourself: "I give myself permission to trust others/be vulnerable/be interdependent with them" (or whatever permission you need). This represents the opposite of the prohibition or taboo which is currently interfering with your behavior.

2. Reflective Observation
Notice what happens. Give it time. Repeat the words—something will happen. Do the words settle well inside you or do they not? If they settle well, then how many more times do you need to verbalize the permission until they are fully welcomed, embraced, and integrated within yourself, such that they feel like a mental map from which you can now operate? If they do not, how do you know? Do any images come to mind? Do you speak or hear words that object to the permission? Is there a kinesthetic sense within your body that seems like a block or objection? If so, then what is the objection?

Pay attention to your experience.

3. Address the Objection(s)

If there is an objection, or multiple objections, then identify them and articulate them. Any objection that you sense against the permission is an idea of some sort (i.e., belief, understanding) which contradicts or fights the new idea that you are now permitting. As you do so, do you judge that you still believe them, or are they old belief frames that come from an earlier time in your life that is no longer relevant? If there is still some value in them, then what is that value? What part of the objection continues to hold some legitimacy for you?

4. Redesign Your Permission

Taking the value that is still relevant from the objection, create a new permission that provides a fresh frame of reference (i.e., belief frame, meaning frame). For example:

I give myself permission to trust people after I have evidence that the person is trustworthy and does what he or she says.

I give myself permission to accept differences because everybody operates from their own mental maps.

I give myself permission to welcome and entertain differences, believing that patience, understanding, and dialogue will enable us to come to a shared understanding.

---

5. Reiterate the Process Until Resolved

Continue answering the objections and creating new permission frames until the permission begins to settle inside you. Repeat these as many times as necessary until it begins to become familiar and fully welcomed.

Adopting the Language of Collaboration

Once you have integrated within yourself the ability to accept, embrace, and acknowledge differences, the next step is to begin to learn how to talk the language of collaboration—especially when it comes to differences. The challenge is that almost everyone has learned a different set of linguistics when it comes to differences, especially those that separate and divide people.

When we differ, we tend to think and talk in terms of right and wrong, good and bad, intelligent and stupid, me and you, us and them. Dichotomous either/or thinking and negative personalizing of the other person tends to dominate our perspective:

What's wrong with you that you think that way?

Anyone with any intelligence would never say that!

Management never looks out for us, they only look out for themselves.

All of this is natural. We learned this way of thinking when we were children, so it's a normal aspect of our development. Dichotomous either/or thinking is one of the inescapable stages of cognitive development. We all started there, but some of us have stayed with that level of thinking.

Here are some tips that will help when you are learning the language of collaboration:

- Use "we" rather than "I."
- Replace, "Yes, but …" with, "Yes, and …"
- Eliminate language that insults or personalizes and use more neutral language about colleagues' behaviors.
- Challenge either/or framing by asking exploratory questions and see if you can get to both/and.
- Replace problem-orientation questions and statements with solution-focused ones. For example, instead of asking, "What's the problem?" ask, "How can we solve the challenge before us?"
- Move from the level of taking positions to a meta-level. Ask, "What frame unites both of these positions? What do both of these positions have in common?"

Another linguistic shift that most of us have to make is from mismatching to matching. When we mismatch what someone says or offers, we not only start with "But ..." which is obvious, but we also immediately talk about what has been overlooked or how the explanation is wrong. For many people, this is a perceptual lens that describes how they look at the world.[1] The good news is that these are not fixed neurological patterns—they can be altered, shifted, and expanded. One way to do this is to entertain questions that redirectionalize our perceptions and send our awareness in the opposite direction—in this case, to redirect from sorting for differences to sorting for sameness.

Structuring To Integrate Differences

To fully prepare for collaboration you will probably need to make some structural changes. These will focus on how people relate to each other, how interactions occur in the organization, and how easy or difficult it is for conflicts to be brought into the open and addressed. In order to tackle these issues, you may choose to use Socratic inquiry and dialogue to help colleagues learn about the new culture of collaboration.

What needs to change in your organization's collaborations that will reflect a structural shift that supports the embracing and harvesting of differences? Is collaboration rewarded or is competition rewarded? As a collaborative leader, do you go first in terms of sharing information, or do you withhold information on a "need to know" basis? Are there opportunities for people to socialize and get to know each other on a personal level, or is the schedule so tight that there is no time for any kind of social interaction? Is bad news welcomed in the group, or does everyone tiptoe around the 800 pound gorilla in the room?

Lou Gestner, CEO of IBM, and Jack Welch at GE opened up the channels of communication up and down their companies. Both men wanted to hear what everybody in the organization knew about any problem—for example, on finding GE focused in on itself, Welch set a new vision and mission: to focus on the customer. Both worked to eliminate elitism and move toward teamwork, rewarding people who helped their colleagues.

1　Meta-programs in NLP are perceptual lenses, similar to the glass is half full or half empty perception of the optimistic–pessimistic dichotomy.

Opening up the communication channels is at the very heart of collaboration in an organization, so anything and everything considered as "bad news" can get heard as quickly as possible and then be dealt with. For most leaders, this requires an increased ability to listen to things they may not want to hear and to validate the courage of people to bring it up.

Effectively Dealing With Conflict

Conflict is inevitable whenever there are people attempting to work together, and especially when there are individuals who own and claim their individuality and differences. As long as there are variations in understandings about vision, strategy, and tactics, there will be conflict about these things. So too with personality, positions, skills, decisions, perceptions, values, lifestyles, and so on. So, the question is not, "How can we eliminate conflict?" Instead, it is, "How can we conflict in ways that bring out the best in all of us and serve the shared vision?" or, "How can we hold the difficult conversations that need to be held and stay together, understand each other, and come to some win-win arrangements?" In other words, "How can we collaborate despite being different and work within our differences?"

For collaboration to succeed, not only do we have to deal constructively with clashes, but we also have to learn how to engage constructively in conflict. If not, the collaboration will fall apart. Few people have grown up learning strategies to deal with this. The good news is that it can be learned—if we are willing to learn.

To begin the learning, we need to see conflict and differences as just part of the process of collaboration. When we do, we will stop trying to sweep disagreement under the carpet or treating it as a bad thing. It is not. It is simply two or more different viewpoints or values that differ. That's all. We can use this difference to energize the collaboration and create something richer.

How do we prevent differences resulting in arguing, quarreling, blaming, accusing, defensiveness, either/or thinking, parochial politics, and all of the divisive things that happen when we do not deal with conflict constructively? The answer is twofold. First, we need to learn and practice the skills of constructive conflicting. Second, we need to organize the way we work through differences by setting effective ground rules. We can then practice our highly developed skills at those times when we really need them—when we are having difficult conversations.

Developing constructive conflicting skills involves accepting strong and disturbing emotions as just that—emotions—and not a sign that someone is a "bad" person. The individual is just emoting and that is usually because we have touched on something very meaningful to them. As a leader, expertise in constructive conflicting includes the skill of defusing—that is, helping a person (or persons) to release the energy of his strong emotions.

You might do this by letting an individual vent and get their intense feelings out. Or you might seek first to understand and then linguistically match their viewpoint(s) so that he feels understood. You could do this by reminding rival colleagues of the ground rules and asking them to follow those rules. This process enables people to disentangle the emotions that accompany conflict so that we can more calmly explore and understand each other and our positions.

Next comes the skill of openly exploring the subject by delving into the meanings and assumptions that each of us bring to the conversation. Here we might call for a meta-moment of reflection to step back and run some quality control questions on our conversation. Here, we want to distinguish our self from our conversation and way of thinking.

I am more than my verbal behavior—my words, his words, the way things are said. These are just words and expressions. I am more than this.

He is more and different from his ineffective communication skills. He is a human being to be loved and respected.

Next come the ground rules. Dealing with conflict constructively involves a commitment to the ground rules so that we can blow the whistle on ways of communicating that make things worse. These are the obvious dysfunctional interactions that typically amplify the conflict: blaming, sarcasm, judgments, over-generalizations, yelling, and name-calling. By constructive confrontation, we mean dealing with difficult issues (things that are potentially unpleasant, subjects that trigger us to get upset, frustrated, angry, sad, etc.) with respect and empathy, always seeking first to understand thoroughly before making any decisions.

Ground Rules For Handling Conflict

Any ground rules that we establish for difficult conversations, or for meetings during which we need to address problems (or potential problems), offer us the opportunity to create a protocol or a written agreement about how we will treat each other when we communicate and make decisions. These collaborative ground rules represent guidelines about how we will work together through any disagreements.

Here are some ground rules for how we can work through various differences and create win-win arrangements in relation to respect, fairness, listening, openness, confidentiality, commitment and responsibility, and trust.

Respect:
- We will be respectful by looking at each other when talking and using an appropriate tone.
- We will avoid behaviors that members consider disrespectful (e.g., rolling the eyes, huffing).
- We will deal directly with a matter and a person; no triangling (i.e., the dysfunctional communication pattern of talking to others about someone without going to them directly).
- We will distinguish the person from their behavior; no personalizing or personal attacks.

Fairness:
- We will be fair about the amount of time each person speaks.
- We will take turns in speaking so no one dominates a conversation or talks over another.
- We will balance advocacy and inquiry: state and ask.
- We will dialogue to understand each other.
- We will establish a relevance frame together and hold to it.

Listening:
- We will seek first to understand and then to be understood.
- We will listen for the purpose of understanding, not finding fault.
- We will demonstrate understanding by repeating our understanding to the other's satisfaction.
- We will reveal our assumptions as we advocate our positions.

Openness:
- We will be open to each person's point of view and position by asking and listening.
- We will be open in sharing information and not hiding information from each other.
- We will openly communicate and make decisions together.
- We will explore each other's reasoning and assumptions.
- We will be open to having our own reasoning and assumptions explored.

Confidentiality:
- We will keep confidential the things we designate as confidential.
- The processes/experiences leading to our conclusions will remain private.

Commitment and Responsibility:
- We will be responsible for our commitment to each other; to be present and loyal.
- We will be responsible to each other for what we have promised.

Trust:
- We will trust that what we say is what we mean.
- We will permit each other to challenge us and/or ask "hard" questions.
- We will challenge each other to examine both what we are saying and why we are saying it.
- We will give others the right to hold us accountable for following through on our word.
- We will manage our own states and take a time-out if we need to.

Ground Rules of What We Will Not Do:
- Get physical (e.g., putting our hands on another person); no slapping or pushing.
- Snipe, zap, scorn, or humiliate to displace our negative emotions on to others.
- Use sarcastic language, dismissive language, or put-downs.
- Talk in monologues.
- Talk over another person.
- Jump in at the end of another person's sentence; instead, we will all take a breath and leave a moment of silence.

Collaboration In a Hostile Environment

Can collaboration work when there is hostility? Would it work in the highly charged political environment of Washington DC in times of partisan politics? Fascinatingly enough, it did during the presidency of Ronald Reagan and the equally powerful Speaker of the House, Tip O'Neill. Chris Matthews tells the story in his book, *Tip and the Gipper: When Politics Worked* (2013).

With the election of Ronald Reagan as president of the United States in 1980, the Democrats lost the White House and the Senate but retained the House of Representatives. The Speaker of the House at that time was Thomas "Tip" O'Neill, Reagan's key opponent in Washington. And while they fought over all of the major issues of the day—welfare, taxes, covert military operations, social security—amazingly, they were able to find their way to agreements and collaboration.

How was that possible? How were these two leaders on opposite sides of the political divide able to get beyond their disagreements, and even beyond parochial politics, and work together in productive ways? Each was not only a leader, but a collaborative leader. Each was affable, practical, and charming in his own way, and each committed himself to keeping the communication lines open between the White House and the Speaker's office.

Both were also able to recognize their mutual goals. For example, Matthews (2013, p. 245) describes how Republicans and Democrats needed to keep social security sound, so Reagan and O'Neill engaged in the give-and-take process in order to make that possible. Both knew that it was for the good of the country and valued "working in service of the country" (p. 251), even though the rivalry was, at times, ferocious. One of the motivations that drove them was expressed best by a sign that sat on Reagan's desk: "There is no limit to the current good you can do if you don't care who gets the credit" (p. 339).

And how did they go about building and maintaining this collaborative relationship? Together they forged a method which became their routine and ritual for staying in touch with each other, and which eventually enabled them to become friends. It was driven by a positive attitude and commitment: "Both focused on creating a relationship so they could deal" (p. 36). Then there was the ritual. O'Neill introduced Reagan to the idea of "after six o'clock": "Despite disagreements, we were friends after six o'clock and on weekends" (p. 37). This enabled them both to be conciliatory to the opposition party. Matthews observes that O'Neill "repudiated obstructionism," stating that "We will cooperate in every way" (p. 30).

When the rhetoric became too strong—for example, when Reagan responded to some unfair criticism by O'Neill and said that it was "sheer demagoguery" (p. 138)—he apologized the next day. That protected the relationship and reconfirmed that "before six o'clock it's politics" (p. 142), but not after six.

Even though they were both men of conviction, and each man embodied the philosophy of his party, they were able to create a bipartisan cooperation (p. 247). They did this by establishing and following their conflict ground rules and by both respecting those rules:

- Give and take: Tip said, "Both sides have to give a little," and, in the end, Reagan was "willing to allow a breach in his no-tax firewall" for that purpose (p. 244).
- Respect: Both operated from respect for the other and for the political system and so preferred to play by the rules.
- Always talk: Both were committed to keeping each other in the loop of communication and were always willing to talk.
- Think win-win: "Neither acted like a spoiled kid" (p. 368) and both believed in keeping the process going. They did not play a zero-sum game.
- Support: "Each made the other look stronger and bigger."

At the retirement party for O'Neill, Reagan spoke directly to him about their relationship:

Mr. Speaker, I'm grateful you have permitted me in the past, and I hope, in the future, that singular honor, the honor of calling you my friend. I think the fact of our friendship is a testimony to the political system that we're part of and the country we live in, a country which permits two not-so-shy and not-so-retiring Irishmen to have it out on the issues rather than on each other or their countrymen. (pp. 340–341)

To this O'Neill responded:

Mr. President, we have differing philosophies, but I want to tell you how much I admire your ability, your talent, the way you handle the American people, the love the American people have for you and your leadership even though I'm opposed to it. … I think of your charm, your humor, your wit. You're a beautiful individual, Mr. President. Thank you for being here. (p. 341)

Your Next Steps In Being a Collaborative Leader

This step is a challenging one because we usually avoid drawing attention to differences, feel frustrated about differences, and so we get into conflict over differences. We do not embrace, welcome, or integrate them into our working practices. Yet this is an essential requirement if we are to truly collaborate. The key to this is reframing difference so it isn't viewed as a problem but as a resource.

So, are you ready to collaborate on this one? Here is your checklist. Gauge yourself from 0 to 10 on where you are at present and where you need to focus your attention.

- I have identified my current frames about differences.
- I have reframed all of the old frames that interfered with accepting, embracing, and integrating differences.
- I have shifted my language so that my speech supports differences.
- I have altered the environmental structures of my life so that they support the integration of differences.

Chapter 10

Integrating Self and Others

The Collaborative Quadrants

> Leaders focused on seeing that problems get solved rather than that their solution gets adopted are key to the success of any collaborative effort.
>
> **John Parr**

The next core competency for collaboration is that of combining the emphasis on self *and* others to create a single focus that simultaneously unites both. This represents an important dynamic aspect of collaboration, and it results in a surprising synergy. Effective and lasting collaboration ensues when these two high level competencies are united. But there is a paradox: The best collaborations come not from passively submitting to someone else's ideas or from leading the way without reference to your relationships with others. Successful collaboration requires both a strong sense of self *and* a strong sense of working together with others.

We looked at the barriers to collaboration in Chapter 4 when we introduced the self and others axes. These axes have two foci: self-development and social development. Here we will go into more detail about these axes and how the interaction between the two creates the required synergy for collaboration.

The collaboration quadrants are created from two axes: self/alone and others/together. Each axis speaks about our knowledge and skills in relating to each one. On the self axis, the steps are of self-knowledge, emotional intelligence, and self-development. It begins from not knowing the self at all and moves to a high level of skill in self-development. On the others axis, the steps measure the development of a person's relational and social knowledge and skills.

This means the four quadrants are made up as follows:

Quadrant 1: Undeveloped. Uninformed and unskilled in

dealing effectively with oneself and with others. This is the
non-collaborative quadrant.

Quadrant 2: Socially developed. Highly knowledgeable and
skilled in being able to connect with others, achieve rapport,
etc., but not skilled in integrating this with oneself. Problems
include giving away too much, getting walked over, and being
taken advantage of. This is the *dependent and/or interdependent*
quadrant.

Quadrant 3: Personally developed. Highly knowledgeable and
skilled in relating to oneself, knowing one's strengths and
weaknesses, talents and skills, values and beliefs, etc. Strengths
lie in being assertive, self-aware, self-disciplined, etc. Problems
show up as being too much of a lone ranger, unable to get or
maintain rapport, overemphasis on the self (and so experienced
by others as selfish), unable to inspire and win others to a
common vision. This is the *independent* quadrant.

Quadrant 4: Integrated in both personal and social
development. A synergy of both self-development and
others-development so there is a balanced and optimal
presentation. This is the *collaborative* quadrant.

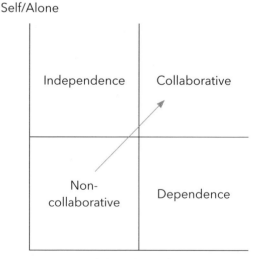

Self/Alone

Independence   Collaborative

Non-   Dependence
collaborative

Others/Together

Self Axis—The Independence of Going It Alone

Here the focus is on the self—on how you experience yourself and your skills when working alone. The scale goes from being needy and dependent, unaware of yourself, and unable to stand on your own two feet to being fully independent, self-aware, and with the ego-strength to stand on your own feet.

Dependent	Self	Independent
Needy, unaware doubting self		Self-aware, ego-strength

At the far left on the self axis, there is little or no development of the self as an individual and so there is little ability to collaborate since the person is needy, blind to the self, and so unable to contribute very much, if at all. At the far right on the self axis, the person experiences himself as a fully developed individual. We know who we are, what we are about, and how to cope with, even master, our needs and wants. This represents a high level of personal development and the ego-strength to take on the challenges of life. All of this enables us to be an independent person and, as such, we have a strong base from which to collaborate.

Others Axis—The Interdependence of Working Together With Others

This axis focuses on the skills required when relating to others. It covers the scale from being unsocial and unaware of others to being fully aware, attentive, validating, and caring of others.

Unsocial	**Others**	High social intelligence
Unaware of others Uncaring, doubting others Untrusting of others		Appreciating others' talents Acknowledging, relying upon others Trusting of others

At the far left of the axis, a person is unable to connect with others, attend to others, care about others, or even give much energy to attending or noticing others. Someone lacking in these qualities and skills is unable to collaborate because they do not know how to effectively relate to others. The far right of this axis denotes the contrasting ability to attend to, care about, and reference others. This indicates a high level of empathy, the social intelligence to take "second position,"[1] and to support others.

From Separate Axes To the Synergy of the Axes

The combining of the highest forms of these two foci or sets of skills leads to quadrant 4 where we find the best forms of collaboration.

As we have seen, on the self axis the focus is on the self, on doing things alone, and wanting to win individually. The following list describes the developmental process and distinctions along this axis:

1. *Undeveloped*: Person does not know self, has not developed their skills.
2. *Know self*: Person knows his or her talents, potential, and style.
3. *Accept self*: Person has developed awareness and acceptance of both his or her strengths and weaknesses.
4. *Appreciate self*: Person has identified and developed his or her strengths and appreciatively focused on them.
5. *Trust self*: Person has experience in learning and developing skills so knows what he or she can and cannot trust.

---

1   Second position refers to NLP Perceptual Positions. First position is seeing things from your own eyes, hearing from your own ears, and sensing from your own body. Second position is imagining what things must look, sound, and sense like from another person's perspective. Third position is the system perceptive—imagining what both you and the other person look like from the outside.

6. *Ego-strength*: Person has enough of a sense of self to let go. Ego-strength means having sufficient inner strength in the self to face and cope with whatever challenges life presents. Without ego-strength a person caves in or falls apart when confronted with obstacles and so is unable to deal with reality.

Conversely, on the others axis, the focus is on other people, on defaulting to what they are doing, how they are doing it, and how to get things done with others. The following list describes the developmental process and distinctions along this axis.

1. *Undeveloped*: Person has not developed social skills, social intelligence, or emotional intelligence.
2. *Know others*: Person has developed the understanding that others operate from their needs, maps, and drives and are uniquely different from oneself.
3. *Accept others*: Person has learned to be tolerant and accepting of others, and seeks first to understand others.
4. *Appreciate others*: Person is able to see, recognize, and acknowledge the strengths of others, and to value the things that are important and special to other people.
5. *Trust others*: Person has developed the ability to take people at their word and start from a position of trust rather than distrust and suspicion.
6. *Ego-strength*: Person is able to face the irritations, annoyances, and differences of others, mostly with grace and understanding.

Quadrant 4 combines a highly developed sense of self with a highly developed sense of relating to others. In this synergy, we now have the following:

1. *Gives of self*: Person has developed the ability to invest in himself or herself to the benefit of others.
2. *Shares of self*: Person can disclose and be open and vulnerable.
3. *Complements others*: The person fits in with others, calibrates, and adjusts to others. Asks, "How can I complement you?"
4. *Gives to others*: Person is able to share, contribute, and invest himself or herself in others.
5. *Shares with others*: Person is able to play well with others and be a good team player.

Testing Your Collaboration Synergy

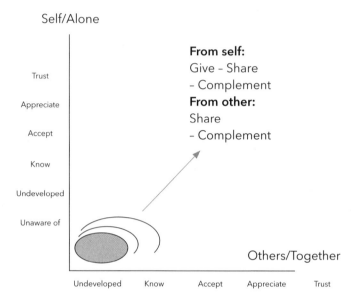

Where would you gauge yourself to be on the self and others axes? To discover where you are in the collaboration quadrants, read each statement below and rate yourself from 0 (low) to 10 (high).

Self Axis

1. I know myself well.
2. I have developed my skills to a high degree.
3. I know the strengths of my talents, potential, and style.
4. I know and accept my weaknesses.
5. I appreciate myself and my strengths.
6. I appreciatively focus on my strengths and develop them as fully as I can.
7. I trust myself and know what I can and cannot trust about myself.
8. I have sufficient ego-strength and a strong enough sense of self to let go of my ego.
9. I have sufficient inner strength in myself to face and cope with life's challenges.

10. I can give of myself and invest myself for the benefit of others.
11. I can share of myself by disclosing myself, being open, and vulnerable.
12. I can complement others, fit in with others, calibrate and adjust to others.
13. I am a good team player.
14. Others describe me as a team player.

Others Axis

1. I have developed my social skills, social intelligence, and emotional intelligence.
2. I know and understand that others operate from their needs, maps, and drives.
3. I accept others by being tolerant, accepting, and seeking first to understand.
4. I appreciate others and readily see and recognize their strengths and gifts.
5. I trust others by taking people at their word and start from a position of trust rather than distrust and suspicion.
6. I have the ego-strength to face the irritations, annoyances, and differences of others with good grace and understanding.
7. I give to others as I share, contribute, and invest myself in others.
8. I share myself with others.
9. I am able to play well with others and be a good team player.
10. I complement others by fitting in with them to create a synergy.

Additional Questions For Exploring Your Collaboration Quotient

The questions below will help you to deepen your assessment of your collaborative leadership skills. They will enable you to reflect on your strengths and understand where you naturally default. They are aimed at personal self-discovery and self-awareness, so there are no "right" or "wrong" answers as such.

Think of your collaborative quotient (CQ) as you do your IQ, EQ, and SQ. It is your "score" for collaborating. The higher your score, the higher your ability and competence to collaborate with others.

Self Axis

1.   Who am I in this collaboration? How do I experience myself as an individual contributor?
2.   What talents, gifts, knowledge, and skills do I have to contribute?
3.   What is the best I can contribute?
4.   How much can I deliver when contributing my best?
5.   What do I want to give?
6.   How well do I know what I can contribute that will complement others' skills?

Others Axis

1.   Who are the others in this collaboration? How do I think about others in a collaborative effort (i.e., as team players or individually oriented)?
2.   What talents, gifts, knowledge, and skills do others have?
3.   How convinced am I that others can deliver on what they have to offer?
4.   What do others want to give?
5.   How can others complement me?
6.   How can others help me and/or us in the collaborative effort?

Revisiting the Barriers To Collaboration

There would probably be a whole lot more healthy and effective collaboration if it weren't for the barriers that block us from collaborating. These are the interferences that hold people back from using collaboration as a way of leading, solving problems, and creating effective organizational structures. As a review, these are the key barriers on each axis.

Self Axis

- Individualism: I prefer to do it myself.
- Envy: Suspicion.
- Fear: Of others winning over me or of getting more attention.
- Egotism: I want to do things my way.
- Arrogance: I know best. I am smarter than others.
- Self-absorbed in my own interests.
- Hidden agendas: Keeping secrets and working under the radar.
- Possessive: Hoarding, fiefdom, silos.
- Scarcity: There's not enough to go around.
- Being a lone star.
- Power hungry.
- Defensive: Personalizes comments and criticism.

Others Axis

- Social loafing, free-riding, not accepting responsibilities.
- Co-dependent (needs others to rescue).
- Intolerant of others.
- Non-responsive to the needs of others.
- "Butterflies" who flit from one place to another, chatterboxes.
- Status quo bias.
- Habit, comfort, familiarity.
- Loss aversion: Over-valuing what we have or own, so losses loom larger than gains.

The Roles of a Collaborative Leader

To function effectively, a collaborative leader must have the ability and flexibility to play several roles. These include the role of convener, collaborative leader, advocate, collaborator, and facilitator.

The first role is that of *convener*, in terms of inviting others to join your collaboration. If you are not the original convener, or even the key convener, you may still play this role to a certain extent. The second role is that of *collaborative leader*—the person (or persons) who sets out the vision and direction. However, you also need the flexibility to move to the third role of *advocate*, so your voice is heard as a team member who can advocate a position, perspective, or direction that is important to you. The fourth role is that of *collaborator*—that is, a member of the group. Without this you have no flesh-and-blood reality within the team and people will ask themselves, "Who are you? What do you stand for?" Finally, there is the role of *facilitator*. Here, you step back from time to time and enable others to be heard as you facilitate the conversation, resolve conflicts, or engage in one of the working tasks of the group.

Your ability as a leader will be limited if you overplay any one of these roles to the neglect of the others. Furthermore, the quality of the collaboration will also be undermined if you get stuck in a role. Part of the skill required to move between roles is setting clear boundaries so that you are fully aware of your responsibilities at any given moment.

Your Next Steps In Being a Collaborative Leader

If collaboration is a synergy between going it alone and connecting with others, then the collaborative quadrants enable you to diagnose your collaborative skills, attitudes, and practices. These quadrants also highlight that collaboration is a high level relational skill and requires sophisticated levels of emotional and social intelligence. From your reflections, what does your self-assessment in this chapter suggest that you need to work on to expand your understanding and competencies in becoming a collaborative leader?

Chapter 11

Believing in Collaboration

Use the words "we" and "us" when referring to your business. Never use "I" and "me." It sounds egotistical.

Michael Bloomberg

The whole point of having an organization is to harness the collective efficiency of people working together.

Collaboration comes in many shades of willingness, commitment, efficiency, and effectiveness.

David Clutterbuck, *Coaching the Team at Work* (2007)

To collaborate you have to believe. Attempting to collaborate with others without truly believing in the power of collaboration, in the value of combining forces with others, is not only a contradiction; it also creates a limitation that will show up in dozens of ways.

So, are your beliefs robust enough to enable you to be a collaborative leader?

Your Collaboration Beliefs

The probability is that you believe in the merits of collaboration, at least to some degree, if you have read this far. So this isn't the place to argue for, or even present, data to endorse your belief in collaboration. Instead, we want to focus on the content and quality of your conviction. We want your belief in collaboration to be robust enough to stand up against any negative ideas or experiences which could undermine it.

The fascinating thing about beliefs is that they operate as self-fulfilling prophecies. What you believe about other people, working alone, working together, uniting resources, scarcity, abundance, human nature, and so on, inevitably plays a factor in your ability to be a collaborative leader. To use the language of systems, beliefs are *self-organizing processes*; they organize all of your faculties in service of them. This will have an effect on your views about collaboration.

What Is a "Belief" Anyway?

Too often, we jump in with our points of view and start debating a subject without clearly defining what we're talking about. To avoid that problem, we begin this chapter with a definition of belief. For some people, the term evokes religious ideas and creedal statements, but that is not the way we are using it here.

For us, a belief is what you consider true and therefore real. When you believe something, you generally have a strong sense of conviction about it. You feel strongly, and maybe deeply, that it is true and that you can trust yourself to it.

How would you answer these questions about your sense of personal belief:

- Do you *believe* you can lead?
- Do you *believe* you have talents and gifts that you can develop into valuable skills?
- Do you *believe* that learning is important and that you can improve the quality of your life through learning?

A belief is a thought, then? Well, no. It is much more than a thought. You can think things without believing in them, can you not? Life would be terribly threatening and dangerous if whatever you thought you believed. But, thank goodness, we can read the newspaper, watch the news, or talk with a friend, and consider the things written, presented, or said and still not believe them. So, while a belief is formed from thoughts, it is more than a thought.

In NLP we say that thoughts are representations of ideas in our minds that we use to understand what is said or presented and which operate as signals to our mind–body system. A thought can be disturbing, even upsetting, but if it is just a thought—and you don't believe it—then it will do you no semantic damage. Conversely, if you do believe something then that belief is much more than a signal to your mind–body system; it is, according to Richard Bandler in *Using Your Brain for a Change* (1985), "a command to the nervous system." And this provides yet another way to describe how a belief operates—as a self-organizing attractor.

A belief functions to attract to itself (i.e., to the person believing it) the very things that the belief posits as true. It organizes the person so that the way they perceive, feel, speak, act, and relate becomes an expression of the belief. If a person believes that nothing will ever work out, that effort and hard work are mostly wasted, that a pessimistic view of life and people is true, then you can imagine how that person will perceive, feel, speak, act, and relate.

It is in this sense that beliefs organize us and set us up to expect and receive what we believe. As a command to neurology, the entire mind–body system is designed to actualize whatever we believe (or, at least, attempt to). This is how we create and then are limited, even sabotaged, by limiting beliefs. Yet, because all beliefs are human creations—that is, none of us was born with beliefs: we create them and develop them from what we hear, read, and experience—we can therefore change them. We can transform limiting beliefs into empowering beliefs.

A belief then is composed of two kinds of thoughts, each at a different logical level. First, there is an idea or thought about something (e.g., "Learning is good," "Collaboration unifies people and enables them to focus on great objectives"). The second thought is about the first thought—it frames the first thought (e.g., "This is true," "This is real"). By validating or confirming the first thought, the second thought classifies the first one and puts it into the category of "real and actual things," thereby making it a "belief."[1]

Collaboration Belief Assessment

So, let's do an exploration of your beliefs for your own self-discovery and self-awareness. In the set of belief statements below, some embrace collaboration, while others focus on barriers to collaboration. One or more beliefs may be standing in your way to becoming the collaborative leader you want to be.

These statements have been organized into three categories: beliefs about others, beliefs about yourself, and beliefs about collaboration. Read each statement and rank yourself from 0 (low) to 10 (high) on how much you agree with each statement. This will help you to become more aware about the frames of mind that govern your leadership style as a collaborative leader.

---

1   There are several belief change patterns in NLP, the one I (LMH) developed is the Meta-Yes Pattern (see Hall, 2000; Hall and Bodenhamer, 2002). Robert Dilts' belief change pattern is called the Museum of Old Beliefs (see Dilts, 1990).

Beliefs About Others

1. None of us is more intelligent than all of us.
2. We can do more together than alone or apart.
3. People want to be a part of a winning team.
4. Others can help me/us grow and can catch my/our blind spots.
5. There is plenty for all.
6. We collaborate best by using win-win arrangements.
7. We can make our association synergistic.
8. Caring about others helps us to grow and get out of ourselves.
9. I can learn from everyone. Anyone can teach me something.
10. The differences of others can keep me from falling asleep in my comfort zone and help me to break out of an insular culture.
11. Status does not determine a person's worth; low status people are fully worthy of me.
12. It's important to care and reach out to help others.
13. It's important to support others and contribute to the overall good of the group.

Beliefs About the Self

1. I can grow by being part of a group or team.
2. It takes a lot of independence to be healthily interdependent.
3. To be independent means taking care of the self first; only then will I have something to contribute to others.
4. I can and will create win-win arrangements.
5. I know my own strengths and weaknesses.
6. I fear that if I collaborate, I will lose my distinctiveness and won't stand out.

Beliefs About Collaboration

1. The goal of collaboration is not merely to collaborate; it is to produce better results.
2. Collaboration can give rise to lots of benefits: innovation, improved results, higher sales, more efficient operations, catching problems early, etc.
3. It is not always good to collaborate; I collaborate with those who can and want to collaborate.
4. Collaboration can increase mutual advantage.

5. What matters is getting the best ideas, regardless of where they come from.
6. Welcoming all ideas requires being objective when comparing the best ideas that many people offer.
7. My ideas are not "my franchise," they are just ideas.
8. We can leapfrog over the latest developments and create even greater ideas.
9. There is no "inner circle" who have special privileges on creative ideas.
10. Sometimes I have to give something up to achieve something even more important.
11. In organizations, we need a solid platform and culture to make collaboration work.
12. Collaboration cannot be forced; people must be willing to collaborate.
13. Collaboration must work for everyone. It must lead to win-win arrangements for all if it is to last.
14. For a collaboration to succeed, we have to right-size the problem and solution on which we want to collaborate.

Belief Transformation

If the belief statements have revealed that you are holding one or more limiting beliefs, what then? What is the process for changing a belief? If a belief is created by validating a thought (i.e., it is a higher level thought which sets the frame for the first thought), then undoing it means dis-validating it.

The most common way to change a belief is to argue against it, but we all know how ineffective that can be. Not only does arguing against a belief not work, it typically makes things worse—it strengthens the belief. Attacking the belief tends to provoke the person to fight for its validity, which in turn strengthens the confirmation frame.

The solution is not to focus on whether the belief is "true." The solution is to focus on its ecology. Does it work? Does it make things better? Does it enhance our life? Does it empower the person? Does it reflect our highest values? Asking these questions, and getting a "no" response, begins to undermine (or de-frame) the value of the belief. It invites a dis-confirmation of the belief's usefulness.

We can then ask, "What would I prefer to believe about this subject? What would be the most empowering, enabling, and positively orienting belief that I could imagine?" This enables us to create a new belief about the subject—a way of thinking that would bring more resources and organize our way of operating so that it has more of a chance of succeeding. Next, we ask a testing question, "Do I believe this?" If yes, then continue to confirm the value of the belief. If no, then ask, "Would I like to believe it? Would it bring out the best in me? Would it give me more of a chance to operate effectively in this area? Do other people believe this?" By eliciting a "yes" response, these questions enable us to begin to confirm the ecology of the new belief.

Your Next Steps In Being a Collaborative Leader

What beliefs do you need to change or refine so that you can become a better collaborative leader? Believing in collaboration is crucial for being a collaborative leader. It is also critical that, as a leader, you enable and facilitate others' belief in collaboration and in the specific collaboration that you're leading.

Chapter 12

The Principles of Collaboration

> If you bring the appropriate people together in constructive ways with good information, they will create authentic visions and strategies for addressing the shared concerns of the organization.
>
> **David Chrislip and Carl Larson,** *Collaborative Leadership* (1994)

To create collaborations, or a collaborative culture, collaborative leaders have to develop and set frames in such a way that the spirit and skills of collaboration can arise within the group. Frames of mind describe individuals' beliefs, assumptions, and understandings about people, leadership, management, human nature, organizational nature, and much more.

In this chapter we will set out the key frames of mind that make collaboration possible. This is a summary of the sixteen key principles that we have touched on throughout the previous pages and which must all be present and operational in collaborative leaders and organizations if there is to be a culture of collaboration.[1]

1. Effective Collaboration Is Driven By Vision

For there to be passion in a collaborative effort, everyone must see the importance, value, and benefits of the project. Collaboration is a synergy of desire (willingness), ability (skillful competence), and emotion (emotional intelligence and maturity). To collaborate, there has to be a strong desire to achieve something together with others, as well as the skills to be able to deliver this as a group. In addition, we must have the emotional intelligence to manage our feelings as we work together as a unit.

---

1   For more on the theory of collaboration see Hall (2008).

2. Effective Collaboration Calls For and Creates Democracy

Collaboration requires a community of equals where we put a high value on partnership and mutual benefit. Partnering is a synonym of collaborating; both terms imply a mutuality that generates a win-win arrangement. This requires a deep democracy, such that there is effective give-and-take interdependency which brings out the best in all of the partners. As we have seen, collaboration is a unique partnership that goes far beyond consensus and networking. While collaborating involves socializing and getting to know other people (networking), its primary focus is shared vision and shared values (agreement). A truly effective collaboration integrates differences and will often intentionally use conflict to deepen the encounter.

Democracy does not mean that everyone has to have an equal say in the governing of a group or even that everyone should be consulted. This is why large democratic groups, like nation states, have evolved representational government. In this way, all of the groups within the population or organization can make their voice and perspective known through their representatives.[2]

3. Effective Collaboration Operates From Abundance, Not Scarcity

This frame is a critical premise for collaboration but it is almost invisible to us. This is because the frames of abundance and scarcity are themselves mostly unconscious. So, rather than asking about these frames, look to behaviors. How do people act? If you want to know what people believe, pay attention to their behaviors—they often speak louder than their words.

If your (conscious or unconscious) frame assumes that there is abundance in the world, you will be quite willing to work collaboratively with others. If you don't, you will feel that every success and "win" of another person robs you of something. If you believe this, then you will experience the achievements of others as a threat to your well-being. This, in turn, will make you competitive, jealous, and envious, which is not a great starting point for a collaboration.

---

2   For more on this see Hall (2015b).

4. Effective Collaboration Looks For and Mobilizes Positive Intentions

Collaboration requires an optimistic outlook on life and on others—an expectation that people are doing the best they can, given their learning, development, and situation, and are operating from positive intentions. This means that they are working to do something good and valuable for themselves. If you believe this, then you can frame the "bad" things that happen as unintended consequences. This might occur if an individual goes after his or her goals without taking the ecology of the whole system into account.

If you assume that people are bad, evil, and negatively oriented, and that "evil" exists in the world as an entity, this means that when something bad happens, it is because someone *is* bad or evil.

Does looking for positive intentions mean that individuals do not get into unresourceful and mean states? Of course not. It means that when someone has hostile intentions to hurt you, embarrass you, steal from you, or betray you, then they are usually seeking to achieve something of value for themselves.

To expose their intentions, ask the person, "Why are you doing this? What is your intention?" This way of thinking does not validate hurtful behavior but it does put it in perspective. People do not behave badly because they are possessed by demons or are less than human. It is usually due to false understandings, cognitive distortions, lack of development, immature short-term thinking, and so on.

Follow this up with the question, "Why is this important to you?" This enables you both to explore your hierarchy of values. Repeat the question again and again, perhaps five to ten times, until you reach a high enough level where you can easily agree with and value their intention. In this way, you will have discovered at least one of the positive intentions that underlie the unkind behavior.[3]

What we evaluate as "evil" (e.g., destructive, ugly, dehumanizing) is usually something that is wounding to our physical/mental health, wealth, well-being, or relationships. It is not good for our values and standards, and because it violates these values, it is "evil" to them. This is very different from the pessimistic view that sees other people as inherently untrustworthy and wicked by nature (e.g., selfish, cruel, mean). To collaborate successfully, we have to start with an assumption of good will and good intentions.

---

3   For more on the Intentionality Pattern, see Hall (2000).

5. Effective Collaboration Requires Diversity and Difference

Collaboration needs diverse ideas, opinions, beliefs, and talents. If there was no difference, there would be no reason to collaborate. If we were all the same, all we would need to do is coordinate our activities. It is when differences in perception and understanding are combined and integrated that we create a richness in the texture of our understanding and endeavors. What another person views in a different way may be what I cannot see because I have a blind spot. Even when it is pointed out to me, I still might not be able to see it. Together we can see more and further than alone or apart.

6. Effective Collaboration Creates a Community From the Rugged Individualism of Strongly Independent Persons

Inasmuch as collaborations create community, then community is the cure for the limiting aspects of a "rugged individualism" mindset. Freud saw the conflict between the individual (self) and the group (society) as fundamental to human behavior. By way of contrast, this collaborative principle recognizes that we are social beings, so living and working together in a cooperative way brings out the best in us individually and enables us to achieve things collectively that we could never do alone.

7. Effective Collaboration Requires Authentic Communication

Collaborative relationships involve joining destinies, which doesn't happen easily or automatically. To do so we have to communicate our visions and values, our hopes and fears, and that requires the ability to be open and transparent, to trust and be trustworthy. It entails that each of us gets real so that we make our communication authentic. No more pretending or posture. To use Susan Scott's phrase from *Fierce Conversations* (2002), we have to "come out from behind ourselves" and be real.

8. Effective Collaboration Is Natural

Collaboration assumes that community is both a natural human state and a state of higher development. Humans are made for working together, coordinating activities, creating cooperative adventures, and tying our hopes and futures together through collaboration. We can easily recognize this by reviewing the great human achievements over time—they were created by people working together collaboratively in service of a great vision or purpose. Collaboration is also natural because of our neurology: in order to be ourselves, each of us is a collaborative network of billions of cells that cooperate in giving us life.

9. Effective Collaboration Facilitates Creativity

We become more inventive when we embrace ambiguity and learn how to live with seeming contradictions, rather than trying to control things or create immediate closure. So too with collaboration. Creativity emerges when many minds struggle with a problem or a challenge. In the process of accepting the struggle, the "impossible" often yields its secrets, and we find new ways to achieve what we had thought was unachievable.

10. Effective Collaboration Needs Effective Structures

Collaborations are planned, prepared for, managed, and monitored. This is because the best collaborations do not just happen—they are intentional. The plan must also accord with the way that effective collaborations are structured; with the wrong structure, a collaboration can go awry.

11. Effective Collaboration Requires Us To Take On Multiple Roles

Collaborations require that we establish ground rules for communication, getting along, operating, and so on. For collaborations to be highly functional, we need norms and distinct roles, transparency in decision-making, good (or accurate) information, healthy debate about positions, no rubber-stamping of proposals, and so on. All of these functions require that different people play and fulfill different roles.

12. Effective Collaboration Unleashes Individual and Collective Potentials

This is one of the eureka benefits that results from collaboration. Through collaboration we can bring out the best in each other and in our families, companies, and organizations. We have to if the collaboration is to truly fulfill its potential. And while we usually do not enter into collaborations for this purpose, at least not as a primary goal, it is one of the inevitable by-products of living a collaborative life. It enables us to play the "bigger game."

13. Effective Collaboration Involves Caring

Can you collaborate if you basically do not like or care about people? You may be able to coordinate your activities and cooperate, but you cannot truly collaborate. At the heart of collaboration is caring for and about people—what Abraham Maslow called feeling "brotherly towards all mankind." So, to collaborate you need to be able to enjoy watching others grow and develop. Caring alone is not sufficient for collaboration, but it is crucial.

14. Effective Collaboration Is Systemic

Every collaboration is a system of people—each living in and coming from various systems. It is also itself a new system of interactions and the inter-relationships of multiple variables. As such, an effective collaboration will be systemic in nature, so we can expect the emergence of new features and properties as the system operates. In order for your collaboration to succeed, you will need to shift from linear thinking to systemic thinking. This will require the ability to see the variables, how they are related, and how they work together over time.

15. Effective Collaboration Gains Momentum From Small Wins

A great way to facilitate a collaboration and gain a sense of success and momentum is to get some early successes. This will build credibility and trust while simultaneously overcoming inertia and skepticism. Ask, "What can we do now that is small yet manageable which will demonstrate that we can work together in an effective way and actually get something done?" As a collaborative leader, plant this question in your mind and live with it until it begins to work its magic.

16. Effective Collaboration Requires a Facilitative Leadership

Last, but not least, collaboration is effective when it is led and guided by collaborative leaders. It could be a whole community of collaborative leaders, but it is more probable that there are a few individuals who have taken the lead—the collaborative leadership team.

Chapter 13

The Bigger Game of Collaboration

> Because innovations occur at the intersections of different disciplines, the best collaborations occur when bright minds from diverse disciplines meet in dialogue.
>
> **Anon.**

When it comes to collaboration, there is a bigger game than just the coming together of diverse people to work on an idea, business, or project. Often, it is that bigger game that pulls us in and keeps us in the collaborative process. So, what is this "bigger game"?

The bigger game of collaboration is what lies behind and above the first game. If the first game is working together on a project that we care about, then the bigger game refers to the higher level values and benefits which accrue when the collaboration results in transforming us, our lives, our minds and hearts, our organizations and communities. These are the secondary benefits that stem from the process of collaboration.

The unexpected gifts that arise from the process of collaborating are almost never the reason that we collaborate. We do not set out to achieve these secondary results, nor are they guaranteed. However, they are sufficiently important—and, at times, sufficiently transformative—for us to highlight four of them in their own right:

1. The being-ness of personal growth as we develop as a person.
2. The creativity of emergent properties that arise unexpectedly.
3. The emergence of teams and team spirit.
4. The self-actualization of individuals and groups.

1. The Being-ness of Personal Growth

When you collaborate, you almost always have to grow. It will happen whether you want it to or not. You will change because of the collaboration. You will develop as a person. You will become more aware of what and who you can become as a person. Within the deep structure of collaboration are surprises and challenges which provide a springboard for personal growth and take us to new and unexpected places in our personal development. Every collaboration grows us because every collaboration takes us beyond ourselves, as we encounter others and meld our minds and hearts to find commonality.

When you collaborate, you make room in yourself to communicate and work with people with complementary skills and unique perspectives, as well as radically different mental maps about the world. This offers each person in the collaboration an opportunity and a challenge for growth. It's not that we become the same as another individual; that would be a form of surface consensus and make each person the less for the collaboration. It is that we expand our sense of reality and our options for how to cope, as well as how to jointly work together.

Passionately engaging with others in a project that is bigger than all of us typically has the effect of requiring that we also become bigger. We grow in perspective, patience, persistence, and understanding. We rise above petty concerns and jealousies. In the hidden power of collaboration there is a deeper paradox: We become more and more ourselves as we encounter the unique selves of others. In the process, we learn how to actualize our highest values and visions in mutual performance with others.

2. The Creativity of Emergent Properties

There is another surprising factor that resides within collaboration that you cannot plan for or anticipate. It's what Ian said one day as we were on one of our conference calls collaborating about this book: "The surprise factor is the eureka moment!" This is the moment when, suddenly and unexpectedly, possibilities emerge that those collaborating didn't expect and didn't anticipate.

Out of the collaboration of minds, the brainstorming and the throwing together of ideas and possibilities, something emerges that is "it"—the answer to the mutual inquiry. It is at these times that we could let out a shout of "Eureka!" Discoveries arise from the interaction of many brains working on a problem which can result in surprises for everyone.

Is this one of the reasons we collaborate? Well, yes and no. It's "no" in that we do not set out with this as our original goal or use this as our benchmark. It is also "no" because, if we did, the very intention would probably chase it away and prevent it from arising. But it is "yes" in that we allow it to happen in its own way and time, without any expectation or demand. It is more of a hope that the creative idea and eureka experience will transpire.

This creative emergence is common when people learn to reflect together as thinking partners and when groups start to engage in collective learning. It is in the process of collective learning, when people use improvisation and openly piggy-back on each other's ideas, that the most wonderful ideas sometimes arise.

The Wildness of Creativity

A fascinating aspect of creativity is that it cannot be predicted. Many have tried, and many continue to try, to predict future creativity—for instance, forecasting imminent inventions. And yet they are almost always wrong. This is due to the very nature of creativity, which is inherently wild, chaotic, and even crazy.

Creativity emerges from strange mixtures of people, places, and events, and often in spite of the intentions of the inventors. An individual might set out to discover or invent one thing and they happen upon something unforeseen. What made them effective was that they were curious and open-minded to the unexpected. Instead of rejecting or judging it, they played with the possibilities and let those possibilities lead them to places that were not even on their radar.

A story may illustrate this best. During our modeling of collaboration, I (Ian) told Shelle and Michael about an event that happened over a three-day period when myself and my wife, Paulette, met with Robert Dilts and his wife, Deborah. We spent time in an "improvisionary collaboration." There was no formal agenda other than to be open to what might emerge from being together. During the time we spent together we were all open to anything and to doing something different.

As we explored the field of that collaboration, it was evident that it was special and unspeakable. It was a "fellowship." And out of it has come a whole new way of working for all of us. New paradigms have also been born because of it. In addition, it revived our spirits and made us better people for it.

3. The Emergence of Teams and Team Spirit

Another emergent property that sometimes, but not always, arises from collaborations is team spirit. It is usually the sign of a very effective collaboration and indicates that you have gathered together a high performance team. These groups of people not only get things done, but also operate at the peak of their skills and have lots of fun together.

Developmentally, collaboration is about interdependence. This means we have moved beyond dependence, counter-dependence, and independence to a new and higher level of development—one of interdependence. We are again dependent—dependent upon each other to come through. This high level trust works because all of the collaborators are mature and developed enough to deliver on their promises.

Because collaboration results from a synergy of self and other, as individuals we are able to avoid the extremes of being either a lone ranger on the one hand or a co-dependent caretaker on the other. This is the bigger game. Collaboration also involves another synergy: the desire (or willingness) to collaborate plus the skills (ability) to work together efficiently. These facets gives us two additional axes (as in the figure below) which deepen our understanding of the experience of collaboration.

Quadrant 1 represents non-collaboration, where we have a low focus on self and others. Focusing exclusively on others gives us quadrant 2: dependence. Focusing exclusively on ourselves gives us quadrant 3: independence. It is in quadrant 4, where we hold a joint and mutual focus on both self and others, that we experience collaboration.

The principle that governs the "desire to collaborate" axis is that we are unwilling to collaborate unless (or until) we see the importance and value of doing so. The desire axis therefore elicits and presupposes the values of collaborating. As we have already mentioned, the key values are:

- *Higher level and better quality results*: We can do more together than alone or apart. In fact, there are things that we cannot achieve alone.
- *Facilitate personal growth*: Complement strengths and support weaknesses.
- *Experience more fun and joy*: With collaboration, we can work together in a collective way that creates a sense of team spirit.

The principle on the "ability to collaborate" axis is that there are skills and core competencies which are required in order to be able to truly collaborate. Merely wanting to collaborate is insufficient. Desire is important, but it is not enough to enable people to collaborate. This leads to a new set of quadrants (as in the figure below).

	High		
Desire to collaborate		I have the willingness, but not the ability to collaborate	I have both the willingness, and the ability to collaborate
		I have neither the willingness nor the ability to collaborate	I have the ability but not the willingness to collaborate
	Low	Low High	

Ability to collaborate

The quadrants that result begin with quadrant 1 where there is low willingness and low ability: we are neither willing nor able. This means that we are incapable of truly collaborating. In quadrant 2 we are able but we lack the willingness. Without the desire, our skills will not be put into action. The potential exists but it is not activated due to a lack of desire. In quadrant 3 we have the willingness but are not able to pull it off. We are unable to achieve what we desire. It is in quadrant 4 that we have both the desire and the competence for collaboration.

In the figure below we have added one more dimension—emotion. What if we are willing and able but not emotionally resilient enough to deal with the experience of collaboration? What if we lack the right state, the right mood, the right attitude, or the right emotional quality to be able to use our willingness and abilities? Once again, the collaboration that we're willing and able to do will not happen. So, collaboration also requires the emotional maturity to be able to effectively pull people together to work as a unit.

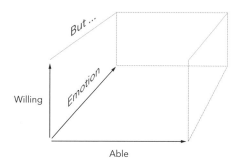

4. The Self-Actualization of Individuals and Groups

Self-actualization refers to making actual (actualizing) what is only a possibility or a potential. To make potentials actual is the aim of collaboration—it is why we collaborate. It is one of the hidden eureka gifts of collaborating. This is because in the process, people and organizations also make real their potentials.

This suggests that one way to actualize your highest meanings (i.e., what matters to you most, your best performances, your best skills and practices) is to collaborate with others on a project and especially on projects that challenge you to extend and stretch yourself. So we ask, "Why do more people not truly collaborate and create collaborative partnerships? Why do more people not extend themselves for their larger community?"

Before we answer this question, we want to point out that there is a significant difference between the foundational "lower" level needs of self-actualization and those of the meta or "higher" level needs. This is the message behind Maslow's hierarchical list of needs:

Lower foundational needs	Higher existential needs
More biologically determined	Less determined and more open

Lower foundational needs	Higher existential needs
More tangible—empirical	More intangible—psychological
Driven by deficiency	Driven by abundance and being-ness
"The jungle" (Maslow's term)	Transcendence realm
Place of competition	Place of collaboration

In answer to the question, we believe that many people are not realizing their full potential. Perhaps they are not living a self-actualizing life and are, instead, seeking to gratify their lower foundational needs. If so, it is no wonder that they are not ready to move upward beyond "the jungle" of these needs. Maslow noted that deficiency (or lack) drives the lower needs (D-needs), so when people live at this level they are driven by a sense of deficiency. This contrasts with the sense of abundance that characterizes the higher needs or values—which is the realm of collaboration.

Since competition characterizes the lower levels and collaboration the higher needs, when we begin to collaborate we are, at the same time, meeting many of our meta-needs. This may go some way to explaining why those who continue to struggle to meet their lower needs tend to be particularly competitive. Stuck at this level, they give too much meaning to these needs and try to make them into "the meaning of life."

For an individual to move to satisfying their higher needs, where collaboration is easy and natural, they first have to develop the competencies to cope with their lower needs. Only then will they move up and become a more self-actualizing person who can live by the being values (B-values). Merely trying to persuade people to be more collaborative through framing and reframing will not work, at least not over the long term. An individual may recognize that collaboration is a better way to live, and know that she *should* collaborate, but unless that person meets her lower needs, she will not intuitively understand the value of abundance and collaboration.

This means that collaboration is both a sign and an expression of self-actualization. Knowing this, you now have yet another reason to embrace the magic of collaboration. Collaborating enables and facilitates the actualization of your best self in relation to others. You and others are engaged in a mutually beneficial adventure. To share with others in an egalitarian way which generates win-win negotiations will seem to many people idealistic and therefore unrealistic. For them, because they live at and for the lower needs, this will seem to violate their deficiency level needs. Yet it actually speaks only about where they are on the hierarchy of needs.

Your Next Steps In Being a Collaborative Leader

Are you ready to step up to the bigger game? Do you have an expanded awareness that many different qualities can emerge when collaborating? You can't demand them and you can't put them on a timetable; it doesn't work like that. The benefits of collaboration are little blessings that appear when you least expect them. And they mostly have to do with the transformations that occur within you and in the cultures that you create as a collaborative leader.

Chapter 14

The States of Collaboration

> People who listen closely are energizing, and people who energize others are proven to be higher performers.
> **Keith Sawyer, *Group Genius* (2007)**

> One of the greatest barriers to this new kind of collaborative leadership is the old kind of command-and-control leadership.
> **L. Michael Hall**

A basic communication principle from NLP is that we always and inevitably communicate from a state to a state. The same principle applies to relationships: we relate from a state to a state. We can also apply this idea to leadership, coaching, managing, consulting, and so on. The state that a person is in—his mood, attitude, space, and/or emotion—powerfully influences his communicating, relating, and so on. It should therefore be no surprise that this applies equally to collaborating. The state that a person is in when collaborating will influence his style and effectiveness. "State" operates as a key variable regarding the quality of the collaboration.

Conversely, there are also states that we can access or operate from that will undermine effective collaboration. In fact, there are states that will sabotage even the best collaborations. If we want to step up to being a collaborative leader, it therefore behooves us to identify the right states, be alert to the wrong states, develop the emotional intelligence to move ourselves from a damaging state, and influence others to manage their states effectively.

So, what states bring out the best collaborative behavior in people? Here is a brief reminder of the key collaboration states we have covered in previous chapters:

- Abundance
- Trust and trustworthiness

- Courage
- Responsibility and proactivity
- Presence
- Openness to others and to learning
- Assertiveness
- Maturity and a secure sense of self
- Celebrating others
- Empathic compassion
- Releasing the past

The State of Trust

Earlier, we identified a basic collaborative principle: Anything and everything corrosive of trust between people stands as a barrier to collaboration. A mixture of states is needed to enable a person to move along the self and others axes and step into quadrants 2 and 3. This, in turn, will enable them to move into the collaborative quadrant 4.

The heart of collaboration involves the twin states of trust and trustworthiness. Trust enables collaboration to thrive; conversely, breaking trust and distrusting others undermines collaboration. The reason is simple: to collaborate, to connect, or to relate at any depth and quality requires us to believe in others. Extending ourselves, even if it is just our attention and interest—let alone our ideas, emotions, needs, beliefs, and effort—means making ourselves open and vulnerable to others. To do so, we have to trust that our collaborators will handle our offer with grace, respect, good will, acceptance, and appreciation. When they don't, we, in turn, will not continue to entrust them with our gifts. We pull back and hold back. We reduce our connection. This will weaken the collaboration.

The self axis is key here. This is because in every collaboration how you operate and relate to yourself inevitably influences that collaboration. As we saw in Chapter 10, the development scale goes from being dependent, needy, and self-doubting to being fully independent, self-aware, and having ego-strength. When you have developed self-trust (at the far right of the self axis) you experience yourself as a fully developed individual. You know who you are, what you are about, and how to manage your needs and wants. This gives you a strong base from which to collaborate.

The others axis is also very important. Every collaboration involves other people and so requires us to develop relational and social skills. The scale here covers the range from being unsocial and unaware of others to being fully aware, attentive, validating, and caring of others. (How developed are you in connecting, relating, and contributing to other people?) A person at the far right of the others axis has a high level of empathy, the ability to support others, and the social intelligence to step into another's shoes. At this level of development, an individual is generally trustworthy.

In the fourth quadrant of collaboration we have a person who is able to simultaneously focus on self *and* others. They integrate their independence and ego-strength with their social skills of empathy and support. Now there is the strength of a double focus on self and others—the enabling, accepting, appreciating, and trusting of both for a solid collaboration. Here a person has both self-trust and trustworthiness.

Barriers preventing trust can arise along both axes. On the self axis, barriers stem from a lack of personal development, self-doubt, low self-confidence, and too much independence, so there is no room left for others. On the others axis, barriers against trustworthiness arise from an unawareness of others, lack of attention to others, distrusting others, and over-valuing others (and so completely defaulting to them).

Collaborative States Related to Self

In this section we will look at some of the collaborative states that influence our sense of self—maturity, courage, sense of abundance, sharing, presence, and proactivity—and provide you with some questions to assess your progress in these areas.

Maturity Rather Than Immaturity

Our ability to collaborate depends to a great extent on our level of maturity and personal development. This is one of the discoveries from the field of the developmental psychology. At first, we are too limited, too insecure, and too needy to be able to collaborate. But, as we grow, we begin to understand that we can achieve much more by working together and by learning how to play well with others. Developmentally, the ability to contribute and collaborate describes those who have settled many of the early challenges and needs and are ready to move more fully into other social dimensions.

- Are you mature enough to collaborate?
- Are you peevish and small-minded about what is yours so that you don't share?

Courage Rather Than Fear

If collaboration is so great and produces such tremendous benefits, what stops us? What holds us back from collaborating and from being collaborative leaders? One big obstacle is the fear that the adventure of collaborating will go sour. People could get hurt or traumatized, and then decide that they do not want to work together any longer.

When there are true dangers and threats in our lives, fear arises as a positive and useful emotion. Then it can energize us to be cautious, avoid unnecessary dangers, and prepare ourselves for hazards. Conversely, when the danger is perceived but not real, the emotional energy of fear becomes not only unnecessary, it has nowhere to go except against the self—against the mind and body.

Often, we anticipate the worst as a coping mechanism in order to avoid nasty surprises. We fear that we will be used and taken advantage of by others and/or not treated fairly. We fear that the other person will not come through on his promises. We fear that we will not be able to bear things if the other person lets us down or if we are disappointed—again. This apprehension makes us suspicious of the motives of others.

On the positive side, fear can alert us to the need to reinforce the boundaries of a collaboration, to establish rules of accountability, and to conduct risk management for worse-case scenarios. Fear may point us to hidden agendas and, thereby, to find the courage to flush out and discuss these concerns honestly. By acknowledging anxieties we can further eliminate blind optimism and come to smart decisions on how we will collaborate. Using our fear, we can test for the strength of the collaboration.

- How much are you driven by fear rather than courage?
- What kind of courage do you need to face your fears of collaboration?
- Do you have risk management skills to ameliorate the power of fear?
- How well can you distinguish true fear from fearfulness and timidity?

Abundance Rather Than Scarcity

The idea that "Resources are limited and there is only so much, so whatever you take leaves less for me" is an entrenched cultural attitude—for most of human history, scarcity has predominated. Prior to the twentieth century, most people viewed resources, opportunities, interactions, money, ideas, creativity, and just about everything else, in terms of scarcity. There was a great deal of evidence to suggest that life is a zero-sum game—that is, whenever one person wins, this means a loss for someone else. This attitude severely limits collaboration. It blinds us from seeing the abundance in the world and the richness that is created in the synergy of collaboration.

Abundance, in contradistinction to scarcity, refers to the sense of plenty. This is what occurs with the higher human needs—what Maslow called the "being" needs. Here, when we gratify a need, the need grows—for example, when a musician learns to play and make music, the need does not go away. It is not a deficiency need. It is an abundance need, so the more we get, the more we want. That's because our capacity grows. Not only do we satisfy the first level of that need, but the need itself expands.

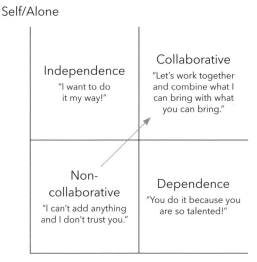

The abundance dynamic occurs in human psychology for those who self-actualize any particular driving need. A person with a need to know things doesn't satisfy that need, so the need doesn't go away—it grows. He or she continues to want to know more and therefore has an expanded capacity for knowing. This is true for all of the higher being needs, such as justice, fairness, equality, making a difference, beauty, order, love, and so on.

Remember, we are always aiming to move along the axes of self and others toward quadrant 4.

An abundance mentality requires an inner sense of creativity (i.e., "I can create more"). Unimaginative people lack this sense and so cling on to what they have. For them, loss is greatly feared. Scarcity often shows up as possessiveness and hoarding, and then leads to the creation of fiefdoms or silos. The attitude is that of a 2-year-old who declares, "It's mine and I'm not sharing!" It is driven by the fear that there's not enough to go around: "I would be impoverished if I shared." People with a scarcity mentality end up living in a world where they dare not share.

On the positive side, a scarcity mentality motivates individuals to ensure that they have enough to survive and know how to protect themselves from loss. However, for this to be healthy, we have to set limits.

- Do you primarily live in a state of abundance or scarcity?
- What is enough? When will you have enough so that you are ready to share?
- Do you have an abundance within yourself or the sense that you are missing something?

Sharing Rather Than An Exclusive Self-Focus

The individualistic attitude has a long history in the West. This has fostered an emphasis on doing things yourself and not trusting others. Taken to an extreme, this rugged individualism prevents people from seeing the value of collaborating. In contrast, social-identity groups and cultures suffer from the other extreme. A person is nothing and a nobody without their group. An individual's identity, status and value are located and determined by the group, not by the self.

The state that synergizes these two extreme positions is one of self-with-others. The attitude of immaturity focuses on self above and beyond a complementary focus on others' demands: "I have to have things go my way. After all, I know best. I am smarter than others. It is *my* collaboration." This egotism reveals an undeveloped sense of self, so the emphasis on "me" is actually appropriate to that person's level of development (even if it is an inadequate attempt to build up the self). The contrast to this state is, paradoxically, a strong sense of self—because this gives us the ability to collaborate. A resilient person has something concrete to offer others.

Arrogance involves arrogating to the self qualities, traits, and talents that we do not have. It is often an expression of lack and neediness. The juxtaposition is assertiveness, whereby we simply and matter-of-factly assert our strong points. Arrogance is a pseudo and very ineffective way to cope with an undeveloped sense of self. It can blind us to others—to their strengths, their gifts, their contributions, and to what they bring to the party. Arrogance is excessively self-referring in that our attention focuses so much on our self that it makes us ill-informed about what is going on out there beyond the self. It also severely limits our ability to listen to others.

For this reason, arrogance causes us to miss opportunities. Because the arrogant mindset discounts others, especially their contributions, we overestimate our own talents and underestimate the talents of others. For instance, in spite of being a "star" CEO Lee Iacocca—the savior of Chrysler—was not a collaborative leader. He was "the crown prince" at Ford when Henry Ford fired him, and his humiliating exit from the company ate at him for years. His second wife told him to get over it: "You don't realize what a favor Henry Ford did for you. Getting fired from Ford brought you to greatness. You're richer, more famous and more influential because of Henry Ford. Thank him" (Iacocca, 1986, p. 231).

Doron Levin, in *Behind the Wheel at Chrysler* (1995), says that Iacocca looked to history and to how he would be judged and remembered. But he did not address this concern by building up the company. Quite the contrary: he worried that his underlings might get the credit for successful new designs, so he balked at approving them. When Chrysler faltered, he worried that his subordinates might be seen as the new saviors, so he tried to get rid of them. He worried that he would be written out of Chrysler history, so he desperately hung on as CEO long after he had lost his effectiveness.

Carol Dweck describes the story of Lee Iacocca as an example of the "fixed mindset." It was a mindset that caused him to go "on the rampage, spewing angry diatribes," so he shrank into "the insulated, petty, and punitive tyrant he had accused Henry Ford of being" (Dweck, 2006, p. 116). This illustrates the limitation of quadrant 3 thinking and acting, where our perspective is entirely dominated by a focus on the self. This keeps us blind to others, to relationships, to rapport, and to all of the other things that are important for creating collaboration.

Presence: The Being-Here-Now State Rather Than Self-Absorption

When we are self-absorbed we are unavailable and unable to be in the here-and-now of the present. This obviously creates a blindness to others and to opportunities for collaboration. A tragic story of a leader who was arrogantly self-absorbed is that of Jeffrey Skilling, president and CEO of Enron. Described by biographers as highly intelligent, he used his brainpower to intimidate: "When he thought he was smarter than others, which was almost always, he treated them harshly. And anyone who disagreed with him was just not bright enough to 'get it'" (Dweck, 2006, p. 120; see also McLean and Elkind, 2004).

This again puts flesh on what we have been describing as the limitations of quadrant 3 thinking. It shows the importance of integrating others-development (quadrant 2) with self-development (quadrant 3). It also demonstrates how focusing on one axis without the other can become highly pathological.

Sharing Rather Than Being a Lone Star

Some people think of themselves as "stars." Such individuals often have a need for high drama in their lives in order to feel alive and to be noticed as a person. On the positive side, we can see in this an attitude of not being afraid to take the limelight, not sitting back and being a wallflower, and stepping up with courage to take our place. It also demonstrates the ability to interject drama into a group, to jazz things up, and to give collaborations more energy and life.

However, when overdone, this can become a form of arrogance: "I need to be at the center of the stage. I am a diva. I am the grand rescuer on a burning platform." The arrogance here is in seeking to solve the issue of our value as a person by the pseudo-method of self-glorification, which often involves some form of self-dramatization.

Responsibly Proactive Rather Than Power Hungry

There is a positive side to power: it can drive us to take control of our lives. This can, in turn, encourage us to develop our true powers of responding, so we can have power *with* others and the power *to make something happen.*

But what if a hunger for power and defensiveness arise from a sense of powerlessness? If we lack confidence when thinking, feeling, speaking, and acting, we can misdirect this feeling of weakness into exerting power over others and trying to control others. Feeling impotent activates several fears: the fear of the unknown, the fear of not knowing, the fear of not coping. As a result, our hunger for power becomes a hunger for external (rather than internal) power. In the end, it can cause us to become dogmatic, unyielding, and unwilling to give in or cooperate with others.

The Courage To Be Yourself Rather Than Defensive

The courage to be yourself involves a basic acceptance of your gifts, talents, and life situation. From this comes the bravery to value yourself as a person and as a human being, and to do so unconditionally. This saves us from needing to prove our self again and again.

When we are defensive, we tend to personalize things that are said and done. This, in turn, makes us sensitive to criticism and too ready to interpret things as a personal attack (i.e., our behavior is conditional). We then live in a state of defensiveness, becoming highly reactive to every perceived slight. Furthermore, our sense of insecurity means we are over-protective of the self. The working assumption is, "I need protecting. I'm in danger. There are hostile forces all around me."

Collaboration States Related To Others

Another set of states which enable collaboration are concerned with how we relate to others. These are the states which support our social and interpersonal skills and intelligence.[1]

---

1   In *Meta-Coaching*, Vol. 10: *Group and Team Coaching* (2013), I (LMH) developed a model for trust in a group. Using seven group dynamics, the trust spiral model explains how a group of individuals becomes an effective work group and then an effective team.

Empathetically Compassionate Rather Than Socially Undeveloped

Collaboration requires social consciousness and social development. An inherent barrier to collaboration is a lack of social development. While we are born without this, it is a potential which clamors within us. It arises from what we think and understand about others, as well as our skills of caring, relating, empathizing, listening, communicating, supporting, and so on.

To the extent that we are dependent on others, as we are at birth and throughout infancy, we are unable to enter into equal relationships which are mutually satisfying. Whatever holds us back in our social development (e.g., social intelligence, social skills) simultaneously blocks our ability to collaborate effectively as interdependent adults.

Daniel Goleman has written extensively on social intelligence, which complements both IQ (intelligence quotient) and EQ (emotional quotient). Our social intelligence certainly grows out of our intellectual development and our emotional intelligence, but social intelligence is both more and different. It is our ability to understand other people, to step out of "first position" (where we see things solely from our own perspective) and step into "second position" (how we imagine things look from the other person's point of view). When we can mentally step into another's shoes, we get through the barrier of being unresponsive to the needs of others. We now recognize that others have needs as we do and that they are just as legitimate as our own.

From here, we come to the next barrier of "social loafing." This is being a passive member of a group (family, club, association, etc.) and going for a free-ride by letting others do all the work. There may be times when this is appropriate but when continued it is a form of irresponsibility. Passively receiving the benefits of the thoughts, actions, and investments of others can become a familiar and comfortable state, even a habit. If we continually receive without giving, we might "learn" that this is the way things are or, even worse, that this is the way it should be. We may then act as if we are entitled to being taken care of in this way. From that dysfunctional sense of entitlement arises an intolerance when others are not at our beck and call, or hurt when we are asked to step up and take our share of responsibility.

So, the stronger the entitlement attitude, the less able the person is to collaborate. She will expect others to carry most of the work and activity and even feel hurt if someone asks her to step up to carry some of it. She feels entitled to be treated as better or superior to others.

Celebrating Others' Successes Rather Than Envy

When we feel envious we experience what another has as an unbearable emotion because we want it too. We think, "As long as you have it, I don't have it, which I find extremely irritating." We may even plot to take what another has accumulated, in terms of gifts, strengths, or successes because of the distress this causes us. As a result, jealousy prevents us from learning and benefitting from the strengths, intelligences, and successes of others. All of this would change if we could accept, admire, and tap into the others' rewards as a gift of collaboration.

When we feel benevolent good will (i.e., love), we want the best for others and do not interpret their success, growth, or well-being as a loss of self. It takes an abundance of love to overcome envy.

Release of the Past Rather Than Resentment

When we feel resentment, old sentiments—such as hurt, anger, fear, and suspicion—are kept fresh and alive by being felt over and over (re-sentiment): "I refuse to collaborate with you. You remember when you made me angry (or some other negative emotion)?" It's like it happened yesterday! Individuals hold on to old negative feelings and feel them again and again, thereby deepening the emotional distress. In this way, we can sustain negative feelings against someone and use this to hold back from recreating a new and warmer relationship with that person. To shake this off, ask yourself these quality control questions:

- Do I need this feeling?
- Has this become a habit with me?
- Does this bring out the best in me? Does this enhance my life?
- What consequences am I paying because of this attitude and mood in my life?

The positive side of resentment is that it indicates something unfinished. The solution is to identify what is arousing the feeling of resentment, and then use the emotional energy this creates in you to take action to make the necessary changes in yourself.

Openness Rather Than Hidden Agendas

When we have a hidden agenda, we are unwilling to reveal to others what we are truly thinking, feeling, planning, wanting, and so on. This gives some people the illusion of power over others because they are withholding their true thoughts and feelings. The premise is: "Knowledge is power, so if I hold back what I know from you, I have more power." These hidden agendas may be driven by fear: "I won't reveal my true thoughts and feelings because you could use those disclosures against me, and that would make me vulnerable."

Openness doesn't mean that we disclose everything at all times and with all people. We can be open and still keep certain things confidential. This is the strength and skill of being able to keep confidences and not blab what you know to others!

Openness also stands in contrast to dogmatism. Many of us today have far too much of an antagonistic approach to advocating our positions and engaging others in dialogue. It's as if, as a society, we have lost the art of effective public engagement. This is all the more true, and true with a vengeance, in politics. Political conversations are rife with conflict and conducted in a combative style that alienates many of us from wanting to participate. It is often too polemic, too either/or, and too "my way or the highway," so it is as divisive as it is unproductive. We are gradually destroying civility and the fragile bonds of community through our public discourse.

Proactive Rather Than Social Butterflies

Social intelligence does not equate to being a "social butterfly." This phrase refers to someone who flits around from one place to another, or from one person to another, or who is a chatterbox with the gift of gab. The problem with being a social butterfly is that there is a lot of talking and jabbering going on but very little doing. The "labor" part of collaboration is missing. It is pseudo-collaboration: Talking the talk but not walking the walk.

Celebrating Others Rather Than Social Selfishness

Social selfishness is a form of egocentricity with a different twist on arrogance. People with this attitude (sometimes called the endowment effect) believe that only their contribution is valid and useful. This arises from a sense that they are endowed with "a gift to the world."

In business this can take the form of "the developer's curse." An entrepreneur who starts a business may feel that his way of doing things and his ideas about the future represent the one and only way of proceeding. While the individual may be socially interactive, and even giving, their inflexible attitude prevents others from contributing.

Your Next Steps In Being a Collaborative Leader

Given that you need to be in the right psychological state to collaborate, it is no wonder that collaborations don't just happen. You also have to not be in the wrong state, as this can also prevent healthy and effective collaborations. A robust collaboration requires people who are open, learning, developing, and secure. It also requires an exemplary leadership state which enables people to follow.

- How easy or difficult is it for you to trust others?
- What is the basis of your trust? Is it unconditional or do you have conditions? If so, what are they? How realistic are your conditions?
- Do you trust yourself to be a good partner in a collaboration?
- Are you trustworthy? Do you come through on your promises?
- Are you dependable?
- What is your strategy for increasing your sense of trust?
- What skills do you have in helping to facilitate the trustworthiness of others?

Chapter 15
The Call To Be a Collaborative Leader

Overall, you need to ensure that your people are inspired and have the freedom to be creative. After all, the success of your new business depends upon your most important partnership: the one with your staff.

Richard Branson, *Like a Virgin* **(2012)**

Do you believe, as we have argued throughout this book, that the call to be a collaborative leader is the ultimate challenge as a leader? Consider how these two terms—leadership and collaboration—are interchangeable. We can define each term by the other. To be truly collaborative is to lead people to work together. To be a leader is to collaborate with others for a common purpose.

While you can achieve objectives and desired outcomes without collaborating, you will consistently underachieve if you don't collaborate. A great many of your inner potentials and talents simply will not come to the surface if you are not facing the challenge of working *with* others, *through* others, and *jointly together* with others as associates. The result? You will live and die with much of the music within you having never been tapped and released, as will those around you in a similar position.

If you want to step up to this ultimate leadership and lead others to achieve a lofty vision—one bigger and bolder than a single person could achieve alone—then begin by appreciating that collaboration matters. It matters that you care about how you lead. It matters that you care about the type and quality of relationships you establish with others as you lead. It matters that you care about the legacy you will leave behind.

What happens when you are not collaborative in your leadership style is that you fall back to bossing people around and being a petty tyrant. The reason is obvious: in the short run it is easier and quicker; in the long run, however, it is much less effective. By defaulting to command-and-control, you will operate in ways that dehumanize rather than respect other people. As a result, you will elicit resistance rather than collaboration—because if you aren't collaborating with others then you are likely to be using them as instruments for your own purposes.

If you have already discovered the limitations of command-and-control leadership (or the shortcomings of the "great man" or heroic leadership models) and you are ready for a more effective style of leadership, then this means becoming collaborative when communicating, decision-making, managing, and leading.

Collaboration is about co-laboring—that is, laboring with others—and being a good team player. Teams can still have leaders but you cooperate with others to achieve something bigger than yourselves and for the common good. No wonder it requires a mature level of emotional and social intelligence. No wonder collaborative leadership requires a great many skills and represents a much higher form of leadership.

When using a collaborative style you still have to make the call as a leader, but you take into account the thoughts, feelings, values, and needs of others as you make decisions. This means that you take second perceptual position (seeing things from the other's point of view)—the foundation for an empathetic perception. It also means matching and supporting the lead of others, hence co-leading. As a team player, you shift from focusing exclusively on yourself to focusing equally as much on others and the good of the wider community.

This is very like the philosophy behind *ubuntu*—that "a person is a person through other people." The thinking is that, while it seems we do many things on our own, in actuality, we are who we are because we have been enriched and blessed by our interconnected relationships with many thousands of people. Richard Stengel describes Nelson Mandela's understanding of *ubuntu* in *Mandela's Way*:

> Since boyhood he [Mandela] understood that collective leadership was about two things: the greater wisdom of the group compared to the individual, and the greater investment of the group in any result achieved by consensus. It was a double win. (2010, p. 84)

Ubuntu encourages us to see others less as individuals and more as part of an infinitely complex web of other human beings—the larger human community. After all, we live in embedded layers of systems of relationships. We are bound up with one another, such that "me" is always within "we," and no man is an island unto himself.

Ultimately, collaboration is about getting value and results from the things that we care about and passionately envision in our world. To do this, we need to learn how to tap into and release the resources within human differences. This is the synergy behind self-and-other collaborations.

Collaborative leadership is a sophisticated art because we learn to mine the treasure (the human capital) within people. We do this by bringing out the best in others and facilitating them to unleash their intellectual, emotional, and personal resources. The collaborative leader enables others to bring forth their unique differences and combine them for a larger good. As a collaborative leader, you are unifying people to harness their creativity and make the impossible happen.

Part III

Collaborative Leadership Challenges—There Be Dragons!

The following chapters serve as a *caveat emptor*. They provide a heads-up on potential problems that can arise with collaborative leadership, because things can and do go wrong. To be forewarned is to be forearmed, so these chapters prepare you for potential danger spots.

Chapter 16
How Collaborations Can Go Wrong

Partnerships fail because collaboration is downright difficult.
David Archer and Alex Cameron, *Collaborative*
Leadership **(2009)**

A sad and unfortunate fact is that collaborations can and do go wrong. Nor is this infrequent—it actually occurs quite often, so much so that it deters a lot of people from collaborating at all. They worry about a wide range of potential problems: What if it turns out to be a disaster? What if others take advantage of me? What if we invest and lose money? What if we fail and ruin our reputation?

Now, when it comes to collaborating, trust is king. Therefore, it is a lack of trust that threatens the effectiveness of people working together collaboratively. Anything corrosive of trust will undermine a team. So, what erodes trust? What undermines your trust in yourself as a collaborative partner? What undermines your trust in others as collaborative partners?

Commissions and Omissions

When it comes to collaborations that go wrong, there are things we don't do that we should (sins of omission) and things that we do that we shouldn't (sins of commission). Omission refers to the elements that are necessary for a collaboration to be effective but are missing. We would appear more trustworthy if they were in place. Commission refers to the things we do that diminish the quality of the collaborative experience—actions which violate trust and contaminate the collaboration.

The Commissions Category

Sins of commission are actions which violate, sabotage, and interfere with effective collaborations. They often arise from negative emotional states, such as fear, jealousy, envy, and so on. They include:

- Collaborating with others for the sake of collaborating or because we are supposed to or expected to do so. The fact is that when we collaborate it should be done in good faith. We collaborate to create a synergy of our differences, to make a positive impact in the world, and do something that we could not do alone or apart.
- Using the collaboration to covertly promote ourselves. This is a case where our ego gets in the way.
- Not making our self open and vulnerable to the collaborative processes due to a fear of close relationships with others or being unable to be open.
- Not bouncing back with resilience after the upsets, setbacks, or challenges that are inevitably involved in pushing forward to fulfill a vision.
- Not ensuring sufficient diversity among the collaborators so there is a poor complement of talents and skills, especially the competencies needed to achieve the objective.
- Not working through conflict in respectful and effective ways, due to lack of knowledge or not applying our skills.
- Operating from beliefs and practices of scarcity. This creates a win-lose framework as it assumes a zero-sum game.
- Not giving others the benefit of the doubt.

The following are some additional commissions that can cause collaborations to go wrong.

One-Upmanship

Playing one-upmanship in relation to others is an expression of competition and comparison. It operates from the assumption that we are competing against one another rather than working to collaborate—that is, using our best skills to contribute to the greater good. One-upmanship also assumes that we are in a zero-sum game, so whatever another person gets takes something away from me, and whatever I give takes something away from me. When we are in a collaboration, it should not be about how much talent we bring to the game, but how much talent will be unleashed because we are in the game.

Silo Mentality

Competition within an organization can result in a silo mentality, whereby one department or arm of a business competes with other departments for resources or the attention of management. The assumption is that we are not working for the overall good of the business but we are fighting against each other. Every department wants a larger part of the budget, for example, so when one department gets more, it deprives us.

When this mentality infects organizations it works against collaboration. People may get on with each other but differ in the direction and outcomes they are working toward. In these situations, the organization becomes misaligned. Hansen (2009) describes the culture of Sony Electronics as suffering from a silo mentality. This created an insular and "hyper-competitive" culture, with each division aggressively competing and "seeking to outdo each other" (p. 8). He states: "It was a toxic environment for any collaborative effort" (p. 11).

A silo mentality obviously works in the opposite way from collaborative thinking, so the antidote is the larger perspective that collaboration can bring. Recognizing that any and every silo occurs within a larger context helps people to stop competing against others in the same organization. The next step is to support those within the organization to embrace the larger frame that "we are all in this together."

Diplomatic Communication

The incongruity of the term "diplomatic communication" is that it is not usually very diplomatic. In fact, it is more likely to be political, in the sense of being manufactured and positioned to create a positive impression. It is diplomatic only in the sense that it follows protocol and (superficially) appears to be "proper," even though it may not be honest or authentic. When the dominant form of dialogue in an organization is diplomatic communication, then it is easy for collaborations to go wrong. True collaboration operates through openness and honesty and by speaking candidly about what is actual and true, rather than trying to create a false impression in order to influence others.

The Omissions Category

Sins of omission are the things that are missing but need to be present if we are to effectively collaborate. Collaborations can die not only from things that are happening which are undermining, but also from what is not happening. Failing to do what is required means that we are not putting into the mix the necessary attention, energy, and care that will enable the collaboration to thrive. This could mean failing to:

- Set forth a bold vision of the collaboration.
- Create a collaboration around a passion.
- Manage the individualism of the members of the collaboration—in particular, out-of-control hoarding, "me first," or "what's in it for me?" behavior.
- Catch a vision of being able to do more together than alone or apart.
- Develop the required social and relational skills for collaborating with one another.

The Destructive Formula

All of this information about how collaborations can go wrong gives us a "warning formula" for how to destroy a collaboration:

- Presume the worst of others. Be suspicious of how others can steal from you (e.g., intellectual property, glory, recognition).
- Assume bad motives in others. Assume that win-win thinking is foolish, unrealistic, and naive and that whatever they say, other people don't really care about cooperating.
- Fear that anything generated by the collaboration will be lost (e.g., your reputation, products, intellectual property, contacts).
- Oppose anything that does not explicitly promote you or your position. Think exclusively in terms of your "wins" and what you will get out of it.

Leading Collaboration So It Doesn't Go Wrong

It is precisely because collaboration can sometimes go wrong that we need collaborative leaders who are up to the challenge. We need informed leaders who are mindful of how things could go wrong, skillful in creating contexts that prevent the problems occurring in the first place, and adept at dealing with any difficulties that do arise.

Leaders need to recognize corrosive trends early and establish a culture that can prevent these from escalating. Collaborative leaders must proactively rectify emerging problems as quickly as possible. To do this, leaders need both the scanning skill of spotting risky behaviors and fraught relationships and the courage to tackle them before they spin out of control.

All of this presupposes that collaborative leaders are willing and able to deal with conflict actively and constructively when it arises. This means acknowledging and managing people's differences sensitively to create a culture where conflicts can be respectfully and effectively worked through and resolved.

Collaborative leaders cannot be naively optimistic, simply assuming that because there is a great vision and great people it will all work out. Undeveloped (or underdeveloped) human nature can, and often does, regress into selfishness and greed. Do you and your team have the skills to address this? You will need collaborators with self-awareness, accountability, candor, integrity, patience, persistence, and a commitment to the collaboration and the vision.

Your Next Steps In Being a Collaborative Leader

Understanding what can go wrong in a collaboration can enable you to more mindfully avoid the pitfalls. Knowing that working with others can go astray in numerous ways, how will you stay alert to this possibility? How will you use this information as an early warning signal? Ultimately, collaborating requires trust in others, the development of mutual trust, a culture where trust can grow, and respect for trustworthiness.

Chapter 17

Pseudo-Collaboration

The Talk Without the Walk

Why is the whole process so hard? There are many reasons ...
you have to let go and trust your partners, and you have to get
beyond the comfort of your own tribe.

David Archer and Alex Cameron,
Collaborative Leadership (2009)

Collaborative efforts require a different kind of leadership.
Furthermore, not everything called collaboration is a genuine collaboration. There are also false collaborations which are often
confused with collaboration, such as alliances when people cooperate and work together. These are pseudo-collaborations—although
they are not the real thing, they often present themselves as if they
were the real thing.

So, how can we differentiate pseudo-collaborations from the
genuine collaborations? Here are some warning signals that your
collaboration might not be the real thing:

- *Talking about collaboration*: Some people use the language of
  collaboration so your conversations about interacting with
  others sound like collaboration. But, in reality, it is just talk. It
  may be exciting and inspirational talk, but in the end that is all
  that happens. It is talking the talk but not walking the walk.
- *Consensus*: Sometimes we seek to reduce the vision, standards, or
  quality of an adventure with others in order to get agreement
  from everyone in the group. This is consensus, not
  collaboration.
- *Networking*: Do not confuse behaving like a social butterfly,
  mixing and mingling and being seen and known by lots of
  people, with collaborating. This is networking, not
  collaboration.
- *A single-leader group*: Some people make the mistake of leading a
  group to achieve a goal or outcome and call it a collaboration.
  This is a pseudo-collaboration, not collaboration. (As a caveat,

this does not mean that everyone's skills, knowledge, expertise, etc. have to be treated equally.)

- *Making a proposal*: Speaking up to make a proposal to individuals or a group to join you on a project is not the same thing as collaborating.
- *Delegation*: Collaboration is not about simply getting people to do what you want by telling them or delegating tasks to them.

Collaborative Talk

All collaborations begin with talk because they start with a conversation. But if they do not go beyond talk, then that's all it is—words, words, and more words (usually in endless meetings). For all the discussion about realizing a vision or dream, this is not a collaboration.

What causes some people to endlessly talk without taking effective action? It can be very exciting to discuss an idea, dream about it with others, and feel a sense of companionship, bonding, belonging, and so on. It is quick and easy. Another possible reason is the fear that some people experience when the talk moves to the stage of action. Now things are getting real. Now the talkers are asked to do something about their words and that can be scary and risky. So they hesitate, procrastinate, and hold back, asking themselves, "Are we ready? Can we really do this? What were we thinking? I don't have the time, the money, or the energy to do this!"

So, one of the ways collaborations can go wrong is that people talk about collaborating in such a way that it sounds like collaboration when really it isn't. An individual could talk using terms like "we" and "us" and set out a common vision, but still not be collaborative. The rhetoric is right but the behavior is not. People praise the idea, but do not follow through.[1]

At our second NLP leadership summit, we talked for several hours, but while the content of the conversation was extremely

---

1   Another set of quadrants are the self-actualization quadrants which I (LMH) developed from the axes of meaning and performance. The meaning axis describes the sense of significance, inspiration, etc. that a person gives to whatever he or she is doing. The more meaning, the more inspiration and the richer our understanding. The performance axis describes what a person does when taking action, practicing, integrating, etc. This gives us the self-actualization quadrants of undeveloped (1), performer (2), dreamer (3), and self-actualizer (4). In the dreamer's quadrant, for example, a person talks without doing and knows but does not act. (For more on self-actualization see Hall, 2007, 2008, 2009.)

relevant and engaging, it was still just talk. That's when Shelle Rose Charvet spoke up and presented a challenge to all of us: "Okay, who's going to do these five activities we have selected and by what date?" Suddenly the conversation took on a new level of reality and moved out from the talk phase into action.

Getting Consensus From a Group of People

Many people confuse collaboration with consensus. They assume that if they are collaborating, then everyone will be in agreement. This presupposes that without a consensus, we don't have a collaboration. "How can we be collaborating if we don't agree on things?" However, they are not the same thing: collaboration is not consensus. Nor should collaboration be confused with a group of people being in complete agreement. This is a formula for mediocrity.

Amazingly, the very opposite is true: Collaboration thrives on differences and, in fact, *requires* differences, which means there is no consensus. For collaboration to be real and effective, it must embrace differences, disagreements, and strong opinions from many people. We collaborate precisely by bringing together our differences and contributing them to create something bigger than any of us. This is the very opposite of consensus.

Ron Ricci and Carl Wiese, in *The Collaborative Imperative* (2011), describe the issue more bluntly when they suggest that "consensus is the enemy of collaboration" (p. 26). They go on to observe that a team "can often quickly reach natural agreement, but when members with different points of view resort to consensus building, you lose the value of having diversity" (p. 133).

In aiming for consensus, we more often than not reduce our differences until everyone can agree upon the lowest common denominator. Reaching a consensus differs from collaboration because consensus seeks an agreement for sameness. It is very different in a true collaboration where we tap into and put our differences to good use by embracing and exploring them.

Networking—The Social Butterfly

Collaboration can also be confused with networking. True collaborating and networking involve interacting with people. Collaboration certainly requires relational and social skills, and among them are reaching out, connecting, inviting, and holding discussions to see if there is a shared vision. Undoubtedly, it is much more effective if this is done with a certain social grace and politeness.

But the emphasis when we are collaborating is putting our shoulders to a shared effort and working as one. It is not just about having afternoon tea together. It may begin at the water cooler or a local pub, but it does not stay there. Furthermore, if people don't know how to move from social politeness and niceties to getting down to hard work, having intense and passionate conversations, and making hard decisions about who will do what and in what time frame, the collaboration will never get off the ground. As Morten Hansen observes: "The goal of collaboration is not collaboration itself, but better results" (2009, p. 26).

Leading a Group

Leaders often gather a group of people around them (or around an idea, project, or adventure) and then direct that group to achieve an important outcome. But a single-leader group, even an effective one, is not the same as a collaboration of diverse people committed to a shared vision. A strong and persuasive leader may call others together in such a way that the union which results is one of compliance (even consensus) rather than collaboration. They may interact and work together well, but they could just as well be a committee or a project group.

Collaboration is about the interconnections and relationships from every person to every other person. By way of contrast, in a single-leader group almost all of the relationships go from leader to each of the members of the group. The group members may not have much interaction and may not be experiencing a collaboration among themselves.

Michelangelo "collaborated" in this way, working with thirteen artists who helped him paint his masterpieces. His biographer, William E. Wallace, points out that he was "the head of a good-sized entrepreneurial enterprise that collaboratively made art that bore his name" (quoted in Bennis, 1997, p. 5). Rather than a collaboration, this might better be described as an effective small business driven by a single leader. It was not a group of leaders collaborating.

Thomas Edison was another flawed collaborator. He "collaborated" as a single leader, but because he was so rigid in his thinking and operating, he could not really value or enjoy the success of others. Consequently, he claimed ownership over every patent and trademark that was produced by the people he hired. And when it came to interacting with others who were equally brilliant, he would not allow himself to be influenced by the other's thinking. For example, with Tesla's alternating current, Edison would not and could not tolerate collaboration. He stubbornly refused it because the credit for the brilliant idea would go to someone else.

Delegating

Delegating is not collaboration (as we are using the term here), even if you are able to get people involved in an activity and take responsibility for a performance outcome. Telling someone how to do something and then delegating tasks to them, while it may involve cooperation and team spirit, is not the same thing as collaboration.

Once upon a time, both of us co-presented during an evening presentation at a conference on the subject of collaboration. When we opened up for the Q&A, one person volunteered that he had been involved in lots of collaborations. He said: "The businesses I run are all based on collaboration. I get young people together and then I tell them what we're going to do and that we are all together and united in this, and then I give them instructions. We have a great collaboration as a company."

Well, obviously, this is a description of delegating, not collaborating. It is a single leader organizing his business in the way he wants it organized. This may be very effective, but there is no mutual co-creation. Even if the leader talks the talk and uses the linguistics of collaboration (we, doing together, united, etc.), it is not a collaboration.

Your Next Steps In Being a Collaborative Leader

While there are many different types of collaboration, there are also pseudo-collaborations which can deceive us into thinking that we are collaborating when we aren't. Here is a checklist for you to evaluate the authenticity of your collaborations:

● Am I talking the talk of collaboration but not actually walking the walk?

- Is the so-called collaboration actually a consensus because we have eliminated differences and created agreement by being nice to each other? Do we have an unspoken conspiracy to avoid anything that smells of conflict?
- Are we, in fact, experiencing a networked set of interactions, so the focus is on having a good time rather than working together on a mutual vision?
- Am I the single leader of a group, or is there mutual working together by people within the group?
- Are we just combining our activities toward a mutual objective rather than creating a true collaboration?
- Am I just delegating activities and not actually inviting a mutual understanding and sharing of decisions?

Chapter 18

Collaboration In Crisis

Leadership is first being, then doing. Everything the leader does reflects what he or she is.

Warren Bennis, *On Becoming a Leader* (2003)

Collaboration can be a delightful and exciting experience in the best of times, when there is a thrilling shared vision and lots of good people whose personalities have just the right chemistry so that working together is fun and joyful. It becomes more challenging, even during the good times, when the goal is less clear, when some of the collaborators do not click, or when there are looming time pressures. If we need to collaborate at times of crisis, how can we make sure it is still effective? What is required from us as collaborative leaders?

Sometimes we can't pick the time, place, or people with whom we collaborate. Occasionally, a problem arises and we're unable to reach an outcome alone, so we have to cooperate with others. When this happens, we may find that we aren't ready, they aren't ready, and because we are all under pressure, everybody is feeling stressed out. So what then? How do we collaborate well under such circumstances?

Kinds of Crises

The crisis that calls for collaboration may take numerous forms. To simplify, we have divided crises into three primary forms: acute, chronic, and complex systemic.

Acute Crisis

In acute crisis, the problem is urgent. It arises suddenly and typically it surprises us. Normally, when a problem takes us by surprise, we aren't ready for it. We feel unprepared because our mind was somewhere else. Then, suddenly, we have to deal with an emergency. Furthermore, we have to cooperate and collaborate with others to come up with a solution.

The redeeming feature of an acute crisis is that it definitely lets you know that something is wrong and needs to be fixed. There is no ambiguity or confusion. Often, crises occur because certain stresses or pressures have reached a threshold and whatever was holding back the calamity has now collapsed and, lo and behold, there's a disaster at the door. A crisis could be about any aspect of life: personal, financial, legal, career, or personnel (e.g., someone leaves or becomes ill).

Now you have to create an ad hoc collaboration with one or many people. You have to put your heads together to accurately define the problem, brainstorm possible solutions, figure out your criteria for the best solution, make a decision, and then work together to implement the solution.

Chronic Crisis

A chronic crisis means there is trouble approaching but it is not yet present. Instead, it is looming in the background and will manifest itself at some point in the future. The problem with chronic crises is that they usually do not feel like a crisis. There is no sense of urgency, so it is easy to set them aside or even forget about them. In a great many areas of life, problems can exist and build up but be completely hidden from sight. High blood pressure is like that: you can't feel it, you can't see it, and you can live with it for years without having any symptoms of the underlying condition.

A chronic crisis can be so ambiguous and uncertain that you're not exactly sure how it will reveal itself, or if there even will be a breaking point. You might say to yourself, "Maybe the signal is just a little hiccup, and not a real problem at all." At other times, a collaboration may have been underway but it has now become stagnant. It doesn't seem to be working (perhaps it is slowly falling apart) and the sign of this is that there is less joy in working together.

Several complicating factors may contribute to make a chronic crisis more difficult to deal with: the tendency to procrastinate because the problem doesn't seem urgent, hoping it will go away or that someone else will solve it, and not taking it seriously.

Complex Systemic Crisis

Another form of crisis is one which involves a system with multiple variables and numerous hidden relationships. In this scenario, any quick or simple solution might actually make it worse, so if we react to the crisis without careful reflection, then we could amplify the problem.

One example of this is a health scare where there appears to be a problem with, for example, our lungs, so we seek out a pulmonary physician. But if the lung specialist doesn't take into consideration other systemic factors, the solution offered could put the kidneys or some other part of the body at risk. The danger here is not having a large enough collaboration of experts and depending too much, or solely, on a single specialist.

The Complicating Factor—Time

Typically, the factor that most often turns a problem into a crisis is time. When an emergency arises, we have to act *now*. There is no time to delay—something has to be done immediately. We have no choice but to act. What can we do now to ameliorate this problem?

The crisis is amplified because, if we do the wrong thing, we could make the situation worse, perhaps even much worse. Merely reacting can exasperate the problem, so the more stress we feel, the less effective our thinking, and the less accurate and objective our problem-solving.

Being a Collaborative Leader In a Crisis

How do you, as a leader, learn to become a *collaborative* leader during a crisis? What can you do to handle the crisis in conjunction with others as effectively as possible? Here are some ideas and suggestions.

Connect With the Enemy of Your Enemy

Collaborations can take on very odd forms during a crisis, sometimes involving some strange bedfellows. We call this the "Odd Couple of

Collaboration." A startling example is the collaboration that helped to win the Second World War. Consider the "big three" Allies which collaborated to defeat Hitler and the Nazi regime: the United Kingdom, the United States, and the Soviet Union. If there was ever an instance of "my enemy's enemy is my friend," this was it!

While the Second World War has been touted as a triumph over totalitarianism, there is actually a very different way to view it. We can also consider the war as a power struggle between two totalitarianism governments, Hitler's Germany and the Soviet Union. The victory was of one totalitarian government over another. The final victory over totalitarianism didn't come for another fifty years when the Berlin Wall came down and the Soviet Union was dissolved.

So, collaborations are not always comprised of friends, allies, or even people friendly with one another. Sometimes, as in the case of the Second World War Allies, collaboration may be created between groups who have very little in common (or, indeed, nothing in common) except a common enemy.

Develop and Demonstrate Puzzle-Solving Flexibility

During the time when we were writing this book, I (IM) was in my home in Connecticut and the well on my property began overflowing, creating an emergency that had to be solved immediately. My plans and the schedule I had been working on were immediately interrupted because I had to deal with this crisis. Yet there was a problem with the problem-solving—namely, I did not have the answer. Nor did any single person who was involved in dealing with it. There were many individuals who had bits of the answer, but no one person knew what was really going on. Because different individuals held different pieces of the puzzle, a very diverse group of people were forced to come together to collaborate in order to figure it out.

It was very much like a crime scene where the police assemble many experts from various fields—every one of whom is needed, even if not naturally connected—and every department or group can call on additional experts. Each understands one part of the problem, so there needs to be a reflective conversation that allows all voices to be heard before a solution is presented and a conclusion is drawn.

This process presents a particular danger—that of jumping to premature conclusions and rushing in to solve the problem. The challenge of collaboration in such circumstances is that often we don't yet have all the information we need, so we are at risk of making hasty decisions. And yet we have to act. So what do we do *right now?*

In every collaboration there are people with different backgrounds who contribute their insights, understanding, and expertise. The art of collaborative leadership is to include everyone's views, avoid putting one expert understanding in conflict with another, and not impose your own viewpoint. The required attitude to take is: "I have one piece of the puzzle, not all of it, and I need the pieces that the others have too." This will help everyone to avoid rushing to a judgment. By all holding back, we open up the space for a more holistic and systemic solution.

So, gather as much information as you can from as many different sources as makes sense. And if you are under a time pressure, do this as rapidly as possible without biasing one source against other, as this will throw out possible solutions and lead to faulty decisions. Perhaps invite some people to play devil's advocate to keep testing the validity of the group's thinking.

Risk-Managing Skills For Coping In Crises

Obviously, a crisis is not the best time to start a collaboration, but sometimes we have no choice. Often, it is the crisis itself that requires that we collaborate. This is when the time spent preparing ourselves for the unexpected can pay off. An excellent risk management skill is to routinely assess what problems could be on the horizon and create contingency plans. Ask yourself, "What could arise that would interfere with our plans? How could things go south? What contingencies do I need to have in place?" It is always reassuring to have a plan B and plan C as back-up, just in case.

Your Next Steps In Being a Collaborative Leader

When you collaborate, it's wise to take time to mismatch what you have planned—that is, take an opposing view of it as if you were arguing against it. In this way you can test your ideas to see how solid the plan is.

- What is the probability that X or Y will be carried off without a hitch?

- Is it possible that something could arise and interfere with, or even sabotage, this?
- What if a key player becomes ill or leaves?
- What if the finances do not come through?
- What if the economy changes?

Appendices

How Collaborative Are You?

The following self-assessment questionnaire is designed to enable you to reflect on the understandings, beliefs, and skills that both support and interfere with your ability to collaborate and be a collaborative leader. Collaboration does not just magically happen, so numerous collaborative skills are required. After all, collaboration is a high level relationship so leadership in this area includes a wide range of competencies. The fuller your set of collaborative skills, the more able you will be to create effective and robust collaborations.

The skills of collaboration include understanding the self and others, calibrating to other people, accepting, tolerating, caring, showing compassion, inviting, engaging, communicating, and so on. Gauge your skill level from 0 (poor) to 10 (excellent).

1. I inspire others to catch a vision of the value of working together.
2. I keep people inspired with the vision that unites our efforts.
3. I communicate a unifying vision effectively so people become clear and passionate about the goal.
4. I build trust through self-disclosure and personal openness.
5. I initiate the possibility of a collaboration by starting the conversation.
6. I establish roles through dialogue.
7. I invite collaboration by asking for help and making requests.
8. I embrace ambiguity and uncertainty in the process of goal setting and goal accomplishment.
9. I calibrate to others' styles and work together with those styles.
10. I am non-judgmental and accept differences in others.
11. I appreciate differences as strengths and resources—I do not indulge in sarcasm or put-downs.
12. I confront the interferences and blockages to collaboration when they are small and manageable.
13. I create a culture for collaboration (values, rituals, processes, etc.).
14. I balance my impulses for individualism and team.

15. I fully integrate both being alone when working alone and being a part of the group when collaborating.
16. I limit and use competition to evoke healthy and fun effort.
17. I think and work as a team player.
18. I use the collaborative language of "we" and "us."
19. I encourage collaboration in conversations with others.
20. I think and speak of others as colleagues and partners.
21. I present collaboration in a way that makes it seem worthwhile to everybody.
22. I make changes that are required for the collaboration.
23. I take baby steps in the process of collaboration so every person earns trust by being trustworthy.
24. I pull the plug on the collaboration if it isn't ecological for all or not working.
25. I set metrics for measuring the collaboration and use benchmarks for evaluation.
26. I receive training in the art and skills of collaboration.
27. I flush out and face my fears of giving up individualism in order to collaborate.
28. I build structures in the group or organization to reward collaboration.
29. I right size a problem or a solution prior to finalizing a collaboration.
30. I scope out capacities which I can deliver on in a specific time frame.
31. I set things up for some early wins to create a sense of success.

How did you do? Being a collaborative leader involves demonstrating a high level of a sophisticated set of skills and attitudes. It isn't for the faint of heart. How excited are you beginning to feel about developing your competence as a collaborative leader?

Benchmarks For Being a Collaborative Leader

Can something as intangible as the attitude, value, belief, or experience of collaborating be benchmarked? Are there behaviors that we can point to which indicate different levels or degrees of development?

For years, I (LMH) have taken various intangible experiences and created benchmarks for them. Eventually I wrote a book on the subject, *Benchmarking Intangibles* (2010). Here is a preliminary set of benchmarks for the process of collaborating. This could be used for your own collaborative skills or it could be given to others for a 360 feedback about your collaboration skills.

The following numbering system ranks the skills from 0 for lack of the skill (or the opposite of collaboration) to 3 for full competency, and 3.5 for expertise in the skill.

0—No skill: Whatever is being demonstrated is the opposite of the skill and so shows no evidence of it.

1—Baby steps: The skill is only beginning to be developed so it will be inconsistent and off-and-on.

2—In the rough: The skill is present but it is raw, self-conscious, clumsy, and calls attention to itself.

3—Competence: The skill is fully developed.

3.5—Expertise: The skill is presented elegantly and is fully integrated into the person and his or her style of operating or way of being in the world.

3.5. Expertise

An expert compliments others; looks for what others are doing right and recognizes it in words; validates and champions others in the team; goes the second mile in giving support (extends self, gives time, energy, skills, etc.); connects people with other people; connects self and group goals; asks about the common ground that unites people; holds people accountable to what they say they will do; and sets up networks with others.

The collaborative leader searches for excellence in others; invites people to be part of a collaborative team; grooms others for leadership and higher levels of responsibility; constructively engages in difficult conversations to address conflict; and uses differences for the sake of the collaborative effort.

3. Competence

A competent collaborator follows the lead of someone else and supports him or her in a project; contributes ideas about team work; takes an active role in team projects; contributes to enable the group to be more cohesive as a team; is friendly and shows good will toward all; acknowledges strengths and positives in others; speaks "we" language (e.g., "us," "our"); asks for (and gives) help when solving problems; listens deeply and asks exploratory questions; builds bridges; involves others (i.e., inclusive); speaks in a sensory-based way that is clear and precise; and does not hedge or blame.

The collaborative leader proactively leads the collaboration; steps up to invite, request, and take the initial risks in the collaborative effort; welcomes conflict and searches for the value within the differences that generate the conflict; and confronts with graceful respect.

2. In the Rough

Someone in the rough looks at whoever is speaking and waits their turn; supports others in a project when it suits them; works with others to contribute to the team; is self-promoting 80 percent of the time; uses "I" language 70 percent of the time where "we" language could be used; and seldom extends themself for the benefit of others.

1. Baby Steps

This person is incongruent when it comes to collaboration; talks about working together but does not act on it; makes promises but fails to follow through; keeps things to themself; does not share; keeps secrets; hoards information; constantly mismatches what others say; engages in self-promoting behaviors and speech most of the time; expresses sarcasm and judgments when he or she disagrees with someone; and doesn't respond to others in a timely manner.

0. No Skill (Or Opposite)

Someone with no skill does not participate; keeps things completely to themselves; criticizes others and what they are doing; competes against others; treats colleagues as if they are enemies; expresses resentment; indulges in put-downs; takes revenge at times; promotes themself at expense of others; only uses "I" language; and buries their head in papers during others' presentations.

Bibliography

Archer, David and Cameron, Alex (2009). *Collaborative Leadership: How To Succeed In An Interconnected World.* Burlington, MA: Butterworth-Heinemann.

Argyris, Chris (1993). *Knowledge For Action: A Guide To Overcoming Barriers To Organizational Change.* San Francisco, CA: Jossey-Bass.

Asmal, Kader, Chidester, David, and James, Wilmot (eds) (2003). *Nelson Mandela: In His Own Words.* London: Abacus.

Baker, Wayne (2000). *Achieving Success Through Social Capital: Tapping the Hidden Resources In Your Personal and Business Networks.* San Francisco, CA: Jossey-Bass.

Bandler, Richard (1985). *Using Your Brain For a Change.* Moab, UT: Real People Press.

Bateson, Gregory (1972). *Steps To An Ecology of Mind.* New York: Ballantine Books.

Bennis, Warren (1997). *Organizing Genius: The Secrets of Creative Collaboration.* New York: Basic Books.

Bennis, Warren (2003). *On Becoming a Leader*, rev. edn. New York: Basic Books.

Block, Peter (1987). *The Empowered Manager: Positive Political Skills At Work.* San Francisco, CA: Jossey-Bass.

Bratton, William and Tumin, Zachary (2012). *Collaborate Or Perish: Reaching Across Boundaries In a Networked World.* New York: Random House.

Cheal, Joe (2012). *Solving Impossible Problems: Working Through Tensions and Paradox In Business.* Crowborough, East Sussex: GWiz Publishing.

Chrislip, David D. (2002). *The Collaborative Leadership Fieldbook: A Guide for Citizens and Civic Leaders.* San Francisco, CA: John Wiley & Sons.

Chrislip, David D. and Larson, Carl E. (1994). *Collaborative Leadership: How Citizens and Civic Leaders Can Make a Difference.* San Francisco, CA: Jossey-Bass.

Clutterbuck, David (2007). *Coaching the Team At Work.* London: Nicholas Brealey.

Cockerham, Ginger (2011). *Group Coaching: A Comprehensive Blueprint.* Bloomington, IN: iUniverse.

Covey, Stephen M. R. (1989). *The 7 Habits of Highly Effective People: Powerful Lessons in Personal Change.* New York: Free Press.

Covey, Stephen M. R. (2006). *The Speed of Trust: The One Thing That Changes Everything.* New York: Free Press.

Darwin, Charles (1871). *The Descent of Man, and Selection In Relation To Sex*, 2 vols. London: John Murray.

Deutsch, Morton (1973). *The Resolution of Conflict: Constructive and Destructive Processes.* New Haven, CT and London: Yale University Press.

Dilts, Robert (1990). *Changing Beliefs With NLP.* Capitola, CA: Meta Publications.

Dweck, Carol S. (2006). *Mindset: The New Psychology of Success.* New York: Random House.

Freedman, Jonathan, Sears, David, and Carlsmith, J. Merrill (1978). *Social Psychology.* Englewood Cliffs, NJ: Prentice-Hall.

Frontiera, Joe and Leidl, Daniel (2011). *Team Turnarounds: A Playbook For Transforming Underperforming Teams.* San Francisco, CA: Jossey-Bass.

Frost & Sullivan (2009). *Meetings Around the World II: Charting the Course of Advanced Collaboration.* White paper sponsored by Verizon and Cisco. Available at: http://www.verizonenterprise.com/resources/whitepapers/wp_meetings-around-the-world-ii_en_xg.pdf.

Gladwell, Malcolm (2000). *The Tipping Point: How Little Things Can Make a Big Difference.* Boston, MA: Little, Brown & Co.

Goldstein, Kurt (1939). *The Organism: A Holistic Approach To Biology Derived From Pathological Data In Man.* New York: American Book Company.

Goleman, Daniel (2006). *Social Intelligence: The New Science of Human Relationships.* New York: Bantam Books.

Gray, Barbara (1989). *Collaborating: Finding Common Ground For Multiparty Problems.* San Francisco, CA: Jossey-Bass.

Hall, L. Michael (n.d.). How to Kill a Movement. Available at: http://www.self-actualizing.org/articles/How_to_Kill_a_Movement.pdf.

Hall, L. Michael (2000). *Secrets of Personal Mastery: Advanced Techniques For Accessing Your Higher Levels of Consciousness.* Carmarthen: Crown House Publishing.

Hall, L. Michael (2007). *Unleashed: How To Unleash Potentials For Peak Performances.* Clifton, CO: Neuro-Semantics Publications.

Hall, L. Michael (2008). *Self-Actualization Psychology: The Positive Psychology of Human Nature's Bright Side.* Clifton, CO: Neuro-Semantics Publications.

Hall, L. Michael (2009). *Unleashing Leadership: Self-Actualizing Leaders and Companies.* Clifton, CO: Neuro-Semantics Publications.

Hall, L. Michael (2010). *Meta-Coaching, Vol. 8: Benchmarking Intangibles: The Art of Measuring Quality.* Clifton, CO: Neuro-Semantics Publications.

Hall, L. Michael (2015a). *Meta-Coaching, Vol. 1: Coaching Change: The Axes of Change,* 2nd edn. Clifton, CO: Neuro-Semantics Publications.

Hall, L. Michael (2015b). *Meta-Coaching, Vol. 12: Political Coaching: Self-Actualizing Politics and Politicians.* Clifton, CO: Neuro-Semantics Publications.

Hall, L. Michael and Bodenhamer, Bob G. (2002). *Sub-Modalities Going Meta: Cinematic Frames For Semantic Magic.* Clifton, CO: Neuro-Semantic Publications.

Hall, L. Michael and Bodenhamer, Bob G. (2005 [1997]). *Figuring Out People: Reading People Using Meta-Programs.* Carmarthen: Crown House Publishing.

Hall, L. Michael and Charvet, Shelle Rose (eds) (2011). *Innovations In NLP For Challenging Times, Volume 1.* Carmarthen: Crown House Publishing.

Hall, L. Michael, Penaylillo, Nelson, Bodenhamer, Bobby G., and Kean, Peter F. (1993). Dealing with the Downside of NLP. Available at: http://www.neurosemantics.com/nlp-critiques/dealing-with-the-downside-of-nlp.

Hansen, Morten T. (2009). *Collaboration: How Leaders Avoid the Traps, Create Unity, and Reap Big Results.* Boston, MA: Harvard Business Press.

Harvard Business Review (2011). *Collaborating Effectively.* Boston, MA: Harvard Business Review Press.

Hawkins, Peter (2011). *Leadership Team Coaching: Developing Collective Transformational Leadership.* London: Kogan Page.

Hayek, Friedrich A. (1988). *The Fatal Conceit: The Errors of Socialism.* Chicago, IL: University of Chicago Press.

Hersey, Paul and Blanchard, Kenneth H. (1988). *Management of Organizational Behavior: Utilizing Human Resources,* 5th edn. Englewood Cliffs, NJ: Prentice Hall.

Iacocca, Lee (1986). *An Autobiography.* New York: Bantam Books.

Katzenback, Jon R. (1998). *Teams At the Top: Unleashing the Potential of Both Teams and Individual Leaders.* Boston, MA: Harvard Business School Press.

Katzenback, Jon R. and Smith, Douglas K. (1999). *The Wisdom of Teams: Creating the High-Performance Organization.* New York: HarperBusiness.

Kemp, C. Gratton (1970 [1964]). *Perspectives On the Group Process: A Foundation For Counseling With Groups.* New York: Houghton Mifflin Company.

Korzybski, Alfred (1994 [1933]). *Science and Sanity: An Introduction To Non-Aristotelian Systems and General Semantics.* Lakeville, CT: Institute of General Semantics.

Krauthammer, Charles (1996). Paul Erdős, Sweet Genius, *Washington Post* (September 27). Available at: https://www.washingtonpost.com/archive/opinions/1996/09/27/paul-erdos-sweet-genius/f3411ebc-ab93-467f-8dd8-a90469031fc5/.

Krauthammer, Charles (2013). *Things That Matter: Three Decades of Passions, Pastimes, and Politics.* New York: Crown Forum.

Kripal, Jeffrey J. (2007). *Esalen: America and the Religion of No Religion.* Chicago, IL: University of Chicago Press.

LeForce, Nick (2009). *Co-Creation: How To Collaborate For Results.* Tallahassee, FL: Rose Printing Co.

Lencioni, Patrick (2002). *The Five Dysfunctions of a Team: A Leadership Fable.* San Francisco, CA: Jossey-Bass.

Lencioni, Patrick (2005). *Overcoming the Five Dysfunctions of a Team: A Field Guide.* San Francisco, CA: Jossey-Bass.

Levin, Doron P. (1995). *Behind the Wheel At Chrysler: The Iacocca Legacy.* Orlando, FL: Harcourt Brace.

Levine, Steward (1998). *Getting To Resolution: Turning Conflict Into Collaboration.* San Francisco, CA: Berrett-Koehler Publications.

Maslow, Abraham (1965). *Eupschican Management.* Homewood, IL: Richard D. Irwin and Dorsey Press.

Maslow, Abraham (1968). *Toward a Psychology of Being.* New York: Van Nostrand Co.

Mattessich, Paul, Murray-Close, Marta, and Monsey, Barbara (2001). *Collaboration: What Makes It Work.* Saint Paul, MN: Fieldstone Alliance.

Matthews, Chris (2013). *Tip and the Gipper: When Politics Worked.* New York: Simon & Schuster.

Maxwell, John (2012). Are You Really Leading, Or Are You Just Taking a Walk? (August 7). Available at: http://www.johnmaxwell.com/blog/are-you-really-leading-or-are-you-just-taking-a-walk.

McDermott, Ian (2010). *Boost Your Confidence With NLP: Simple Techniques For a More Confident and Successful You.* London: Piatkus.

McGregor, Douglas (2006). *The Human Side of Enterprise*, annotated edn. New York: McGraw-Hill.

McLean, Bethany and Elkind, Peter (2004). *The Smartest Guys In the Room: The Amazing Rise and Scandalous Fall of Enron*. New York: Penguin.

McLeod, Angus (2009). *Me, Myself, My Team: How To Become An Effective Team Player Using NLP.* Carmarthen: Crown House Publishing.

Moral, Michel and Abbott, Geoffrey (eds) (2009). *The Routledge Companion To International Business Coaching.* London: Routledge.

Novak, William (1984). *Iacocca: An Autobiography.* New York: Bantam Books.

Otto, Herbert A. (1973). *Group Methods To Actualize Human Potential: A Handbook.* Beverly Hills, CA: Holistic Press.

Palca, Joe (2013). All Charged Up: Engineers Create a Battery Made of Wood, *NPR* (July 13). Available at: http://www.npr.org/2013/07/17/200782520/all-charged-up-engineers-create-a-battery-made-of-wood.

Peck, M. Scott (1987). *The Different Drum: Community-Making and Peace.* New York: Touchstone Books.

Putz, Gregory Bryan (2002). *Facilitation Skills: Helping Groups Make Decisions.* Bountiful, UT: Deep Space Technology Co.

Ricci, Ron and Wiese, Carl (2011). *The Collaborative Imperative: Executive Strategies For Unlocking Your Organization's True Potential.* San Jose, CA: Cisco Systems.

Rilling, James A., Gutman, David, Zeh, Thorsten R., Pagnoni, Guiseppe, Berns, Gregory S., and Kilts, Clinton D. (2002). A Neural Basis for Social Cooperation, *Neuron* 35(2): 395–405.

Rogers, Carl (1961). *On Becoming a Person: A Therapist's View of Psychotherapy.* London: Constable.

Roosevelt, Eleanor (2012 [1960]). *You Learn By Living: Eleven Keys for a More Fulfilling Life*, 50th anniversary edn. New York: Harper Perennial.

Sawyer, Keith (2007). *Group Genius: The Creative Power of Collaboration.* New York: Basic Books.

Schutz, Will (1967). *Joy: Expanding Human Awareness.* New York: Grove Press.

Scott, Susan (2002). *Fierce Conversations: Achieving Success At Work and In Life, One Conversation At a Time.* New York: Viking.

Senge, Peter M. (1990). *The Fifth Discipline: The Art and Practice of the Learning Organization.* New York: Doubleday Currency.

Simmons, Annette (1999). *A Safe Place For Dangerous Truths: Using Dialogue To Overcome Fear and Distrust At Work.* New York: AMACOM.

Stengel, Richard (2010). *Mandela's Way: Lessons On Life, Love and Courage.* New York: Crown Publishing.

Tubbs, Stewart L. (1984). *A Systems Approach To Small Group Interaction.* New York: Random House.

Winer, Michael and Ray, Karen (2003). *Collaboration Handbook: Creating, Sustaining, and Enjoying the Journey.* Saint Paul, MN: Amherst Wilder Foundation.

About the Authors

Ian McDermott

Ian McDermott specializes in giving people the skills to innovate their *own* collaborative leadership solutions. Much of his time is spent advising senior leaders worldwide, and coaching the next generation to be innovative leaders.

Ian is an Honorary Fellow of Exeter University Business School where his focus is on leadership, innovation and entrepreneurship. He is Dean of Innovation and Learning for the Purposeful Planning Institute in the US, and his work is featured in the Open University's MBA course 'Creativity, Innovation and Change'. Ian is External Faculty at Henley Business School where he helped create the MSc in Coaching and Behavioral Change. He is also a UKCP-registered psychotherapist.

Ian McDermott has pioneered Leadership and Innovation Coaching, has trained a generation of coaches, is a member of the Association for Coaching's Global Advisory Panel and is AC Global Ambassador for Innovation and Collaboration.

Based in the UK and the US, he is an acknowledged thought leader. A published authority, he has authored and co-authored fifteen books on systems thinking, NLP and coaching. Titles include *The Art of Systems Thinking, Principles of NLP* and *The Coaching Bible.*

Ian's primary focus is on delivering practical "how to's" to ensure that learning in leadership and change, innovation and collaboration really happen. That's why he set up International Teaching Seminars (ITS).

Over 25 years on, ITS continues to pioneer the application of practical techniques, which are grounded in sound neuroscience, for individuals, teams and organizations.

Contact Ian:

For details of consultancy, coaching and training visit: www.itsnlp.com
At ITS: info@itsnlp.com
Via LinkedIn: https://uk.linkedin.com/in/ianemcdermott

Books

McDermott, Ian (2010). *Boost Your Confidence.* London: Piatkus.

McDermott, Ian and Jago, Wendy (2005). *The Coaching Bible.* London: Piatkus.

McDermott, Ian and Jago, Wendy (2003). *Your Inner Coach.* London: Piatkus.

McDermott, Ian and Jago, Wendy (2001). *The NLP Coach.* London: Piatkus.

McDermott, Ian and Jago, Wendy (2001). *Brief NLP Therapy.* London: Sage.

McDermott, Ian and O'Connor, Joseph (2001). *First Directions NLP.* London: Thorsons.

McDermott, Ian and Shircore, Ian (1999). *Manage Yourself, Manage Your Life.* London: Piatkus.

McDermott, Ian and Shircore, Ian (1998). *NLP and the New Manager.* London: Texere.

McDermott, Ian and O'Connor, Joseph (1996). *The Art of Systems Thinking.* London: Thorsons.

McDermott, Ian and O'Connor, Joseph (1996). *NLP and Health.* London: Thorsons.

McDermott, Ian and O'Connor, Joseph (1996). *Practical NLP for Managers.* London: Gower.

McDermott, Ian and O'Connor, Joseph (1996). *Principles of NLP.* London: Thorsons.

McDermott, Ian, O'Connor, Joseph, et al. (1996). *Take Control of Your Life.* Amsterdam: Time-Life.

McDermott, Ian, O'Connor, Joseph, et al. (1995). *Develop Your Leadership Qualities.* Amsterdam: Time-Life.

L. Michael Hall, PhD

L. Michael Hall is a visionary leader in the field of NLP and Neuro-Semantics and a modeler of human excellence. Searching out and modeling the structure of human excellence, he then turns that information into models, patterns, training manuals, and books. With his several businesses, Michael is also an entrepreneur and an international trainer.

His doctorate is in the cognitive-behavioral sciences from Union Institute University. For two decades he has worked as a psychotherapist in Colorado. When he found NLP in 1986, he studied and then worked with Richard Bandler. Later, when studying and modeling resilience, he developed the Meta-States Model that launched the field of Neuro-Semantics. He co-created the International Society of Neuro-Semantics (ISNS) with Dr. Bob Bodenhamer. He has written more than forty books, many best-sellers in the field of NLP.

Applying NLP to coaching, he created the Meta-Coach System, which was co-developed with Michelle Duval (2003–2007); he co-founded the Meta-Coach Foundation (2003); created the Self-Actualization Quadrants (2004); and launched the New Human Potential Movement (2005).

Websites

www.neurosemantics.com
www.meta-coaching.org

www.self-actualizing.org
www.metacoachfoundation.org

Books

NLP and Neuro-Semantics

Hall, L. Michael (1996). *Becoming A More Ferocious Presenter*. Clifton, CO: Neuro-Semantics Publications.

Hall, L. Michael (1996). *Languaging: The Linguistics of Psychotherapy*. Grand Junction, CO: Empowerment Technologies.

Hall, L. Michael (1996). *The Spirit of NLP: The Process, Meaning and Criteria for Mastering NLP*. Carmarthen: Crown House Publishing.

Hall, L. Michael (1997–1999). *Meta-State Magic: Meta-State Journal*. Grand Junction, CO: Empowerment Technologies.

Hall, L. Michael (2000 [1995]). *Meta-States: Mastering the Higher Levels of Mind*. Clifton, CO: Neuro-Semantics Publications.

Hall, L. Michael (2000 [1996]). *Dragon Slaying: Dragons Into Princes*. Clifton, CO: Neuro-Semantics Publications.

Hall, L. Michael (2000). *The Secrets of Personal Mastery: Advanced Techniques for Accessing Your Higher Levels of Consciousness*. Carmarthen: Crown House Publishing.

Hall, L. Michael (2001). *Communication Magic: Exploring the Structure and Meaning of Language*. Carmarthen: Crown House Publishing. Originally titled: *The Secrets of Magic* (1998).

Hall, L. Michael (2001). *Games Business Experts Play: Winning At the Games of Business*. Carmarthen: Crown House Publishing.

Hall, L. Michael (2001). *Games Fit and Slim People Play: Winning the Fit and Slim Game*. Clifton, CO: Neuro-Semantics Publications.

Hall, L. Michael (2001 [1997]). *NLP: Going Meta—Advance Modeling Using Meta-Levels*. Clifton, CO: Neuro-Semantics Publications.

Hall, L. Michael (2002). *The Bateson Report*. Grand Junction, CO: Empowerment Technologies.

Hall, L. Michael (2002). *Make It So! Closing the Knowing-Doing Gap*. Grand Junction, CO: Empowerment Technologies.

Hall, L. Michael (2002). *Master Practitioner Course*, Vol. 2: *User's Manual of the Brain*. Carmarthen: Crown House Publishing.

Hall, L. Michael (2002). *Movie Mind: Directing Your Mental Cinemas*. Clifton, CO: Neuro-Semantics Publications.

Hall, L. Michael (2003). *The Matrix Model: Neuro-Semantics and the Construction of Meaning.* Grand Junction, CO: Empowerment Technologies.

Hall, L. Michael (2003). *Propulsion Systems.* Grand Junction, CO: Empowerment Technologies.

Hall, L. Michael (2003). *Source Book of Magic*, Vol. 2: *Neuro-Semantic Patterns.* Grand Junction, CO: Empowerment Technologies.

Hall, L. Michael (2004). *Games Great Lovers Play.* Clifton, CO: Neuro-Semantics Publications.

Hall, L. Michael (2007). *Unleashed: How To Unleash Potentials for Peak Performances.* Grand Junction, CO: Empowerment Technologies.

Hall, L. Michael (2007). *Winning the Inner Game: Mastering the Inner Game For Peak Performance.* Carmarthen: Crown House Publishing. Originally titled: *Frame Games* (2000).

Hall, L. Michael (2008). *Self-Actualization Psychology: The Positive Psychology of Human Nature's Bright Side.* Clifton, CO: Neuro-Semantics Publications.

Hall, L. Michael (2009). *Meta-Coaching*, Vol. 5: *Achieving Peak Performance.* Clifton, CO: Neuro-Semantics Publications.

Hall, L. Michael (2009). *Unleashing Leadership: Self-Actualizing Leaders and Companies.* Clifton, CO: Neuro-Semantics Publications.

Hall, L. Michael (2010). *The Crucible and the Fires of Change.* Clifton, CO: Neuro-Semantics Publications.

Hall, L. Michael (2010). *Inside-Out Wealth: Holistic Wealth Creation.* Clifton, CO: Neuro-Semantics Publications.

Hall, L. Michael (2011). *Meta-Coaching*, Vol. 8: *Benchmarking: The Art of Measuring the Unquantifiable.* Clifton, CO: Neuro-Semantics Publications.

Hall, L. Michael (2011). *Neuro-Semantics: Actualizing Meaning and Performance.* Clifton, CO: Neuro-Semantics Publications.

Hall, L. Michael (2012). *Meta-Coaching*, Vol. 9: *Systemic Coaching: Coaching the Whole Person With Meta-Coaching.* Clifton, CO: Neuro-Semantics Publications.

Hall, L. Michael (2013). *Meta-Coaching*, Vol. 10: *Group and Team Coaching.* Clifton, CO: Neuro-Semantics Publications.

Hall, L. Michael (2015). *Meta-Coaching*, Vol. 1: *Coaching Change: The Axes of Change*, 2nd edn. Clifton, CO: Neuro-Semantics Publications.

Hall, L. Michael (2015). *Meta-Coaching*, Vol. 12: *Political Coaching: Self-Actualizing Politics and Politicians.* Clifton, CO: Neuro-Semantics Publications.

Hall, L. Michael (2015). *Meta-Coaching*, Vol. 13: *The Meta-Coaching System: Systemic Coaching At Its Best.* Clifton, CO: Neuro-Semantics Publications.

Hall, L. Michael with Belnap, Barbara P. (2004 [1997]). *The Source Book of Magic: A Comprehensive Guide To NLP Change Patterns*, 2nd rev. edn. Carmarthen: Crown House Publishing.

Hall, L. Michael and Bodenhamer, Bob G. (1997). *Time-Lining: Advance Time-Line Processes.* Cupertino, CA: Meta Publications.

Hall, L. Michael and Bodenhamer, Bob G. (1999). *User's Manual of the Brain*, Vol. 1: *Mastering Systemic NLP.* Carmarthen: Crown House Publishing.

Hall, L. Michael and Bodenhamer, Bob G. (2001). *Games for Mastering Fear.* Grand Junction, CO: Empowerment Technologies.

Hall, L. Michael with Bodenhamer, Bob G. (2002). *Sub-Modalities Going Meta: Cinematic Frames for Semantic Magic.* Clifton, CO: Neuro-Semantic Publications. Originally titled: *The Structure of Excellence* (1999).

Hall, L. Michael with Bodenhamer, Bob G. (2005 [1997]). *Figuring Out People: Reading People Using Meta-Programs.* Carmarthen: Crown House Publishing.

Hall, L. Michael with Bodenhamer, Bob G. (2005 [1997]). *Mind-Lines: Lines For Changing Minds.* Clifton, CO: Neuro-Semantic Publications.

Hall, L. Michael and Bodenhamer, Bob G. (2006 [1997]). *Patterns For Renewing the Mind: Christian Communicating and Counseling Using NLP and Neuro-Semantics.* Clifton, CO: Neuro-Semantic Publications.

Hall, L. Michael and Bodenhamer, Bob G., Bolstad, Richard, and Hamblett, Margot (2001). *The Structure of Personality: Modeling "Personality" Using NLP and Neuro-Semantics.* Carmarthen: Crown House Publishing.

Hall, L. Michael and Charvet, Shelle Rose (eds) (2011). *Innovations In NLP For Challenging Times: Volume 1.* Carmarthen: Crown House Publishing.

Hall, L. Michael and Duval, Michelle (2004). *Meta-Coaching,* Vol. 1: *Coaching Change.* Clifton, CO: Neuro-Semantics Publications.

Hall, L. Michael, Duval, Michelle, and Dilts, Robert (2010 [2004]). *Meta-Coaching,* Vol. 2: *Coaching Conversations For Transformational Change.* Clifton, CO: Neuro-Semantics Publications.

Hall, L. Michael and Lederer, Debra (1999). *Instant Relaxation: How To Reduce Stress At Work, At Home and In Your Daily Life.* Carmarthen: Crown House Publishing.

Hall, L. Michael with Richardson, Graham (2014). *Meta-Coaching,* Vol. 11: *Executive Coaching: Facilitating Excellence In the C-Suite.* Clifton, CO: Neuro-Semantics Publications.

Hall, L. Michael, Seymour, John, and Gray, Richard (in press). *The Field of NLP.*

Other books

Hall, L. Michael (1985). *Emotions: Sometimes I Have Them/Sometimes They Have Me.* St Louis, MO: Good-News Encounters.

Hall, L. Michael (1987). *Motivation: How To Be a Positive Influence In a Negative World.* Grand Junction, CO: Empowerment Technologies.

Hall, L. Michael (1987). *Speak Up, Speak Clear, Speak Kind.* Grand Junction, CO: Empowerment Technologies.

Hall, L. Michael (1996). *Apocalypse Then (Not Now): Indexing the Apocalypse.* Grand Junction, CO: Empowerment Technologies. Originally titled: *Millennial Madness* (1992).

Hall, L. Michael (1996). *Over My Dead Body.* Grand Junction, CO: Empowerment Technologies.

Order books from:

Neuro-Semantic Publications (NSP)
P.O. Box 8, Clifton, CO. 81520, USA
Tel: +1(970) 523 7877

Index